Nelson Literacy

Series Authors
Karen Hume
Brad Ledgerwood

Series Consultants
Jennette MacKenzie, *Senior Consultant*
Damian Cooper, *Assessment*
James Coulter, *Assessment and Instruction*
Gayle Gregory, *Differentiated Instruction*
Ruth McQuirter Scott, *Word Study*

Series Writing Team
James Coulter, *Assessment*
Kathy Lazarovits, *ELL/ESL*
Liz Powell, *Instruction*
Sue Quennell, *Word Study*
Janet Lee Stinson, *Instruction*
Michael Stubitsch, *Instruction*

Subject and Specialist Reviewers
Mary Baratto, *The Arts*
Rachel Cooke, *Metacognition*
Phil Davison, *Media Literacy*
Graham Draper, *Geography*
Ian Esquivel, *Media Literacy*
Martin Gabber, *Science and Technology*
Cathy Hall, *Mathematics*
Jan Haskings-Winner, *History*
Dan Koenig, *Health*
Kathy Lazarovits, *ELL/ESL*
Janet Lee Stinson, *Media Literacy*

NELSON / EDUCATION

NELSON EDUCATION

Nelson Literacy 7b

Director of Publishing
Kevin Martindale

Director of Publishing, Literacy
Joe Banel

Executive Managing Editor, Development
Darleen Rotozinski

Senior Product Manager
Mark Cressman

Senior Program Manager
Diane Robitaille

Developmental Editors
Gillian Scobie
Marilyn Wilson

Researcher
Catherine Rondina

Assistant Editor
Corry Codner

Bias Reviewer
Nancy Christoffer

Editorial Assistants
Adam Rennie
Kristen Sanchioni

Executive Director, Content and Media Production
Renate McCloy

Director, Content and Media Production
Carol Martin

Senior Content Production Editor
Laurie Thomas

Content Production Editor
Natalie Russell

Proofreader
Elizabeth D'Anjou

Production Manager
Helen Jager Locsin

Production Coordinator
Vicki Black

Director, Asset Management Services
Vicki Gould

Design Director
Ken Phipps

Managing Designer
Sasha Moroz

Series Design
Sasha Moroz

Series Wordmark
Sasha Moroz

Cover Design
Sasha Moroz
Glenn Toddun

Interior Design
Carianne Bauldry
Jarrel Breckon
Nicole Dimson
Courtney Hellam
Jennifer Laing
Eugene Lo
Sasha Moroz
Peter Papayanakis
Jan John Rivera
Carrie Scherkus
Industrial Strength

Art Buyer
Suzanne Peden

Compositor
Courtney Hellam

Photo Research and Permissions
Nicola Winstanley

Printer
Transcontinental Printing

Advisers and Reviewers

Gwen Babcock

Jennifer Bach

Karen Beamish

Mary Cairo

Joanna Cascioli

Vivian Collyer

Anne Converset

Rachel Cooke

Phil Davison

Lori Driussi

Judy Dunn

Eileen Eby

Ian Esquivel

Patty Friedrich

Anna Filice-Gagliardi

Charmaine Graves

Colleen Hayward

Brenda Lightburn

Andrew Locker

Susan MacDonald

Anne Marie McDonald

Selina Millar

Wanda Mills-Boone

Lorellie Munson

Barb Muron

Linda O'Reilly

Cathy Pollock

Gina Rae

Susan Stevens

Janet Lee Stinson

Melisa Strimas

Laurie Townshend

Tracy Toyama

Deborah Tranton-Waghorn

Ann Varty

Ruth Wiebe

Nadia Young

CONTENTS

Unit 3 — Mysteries

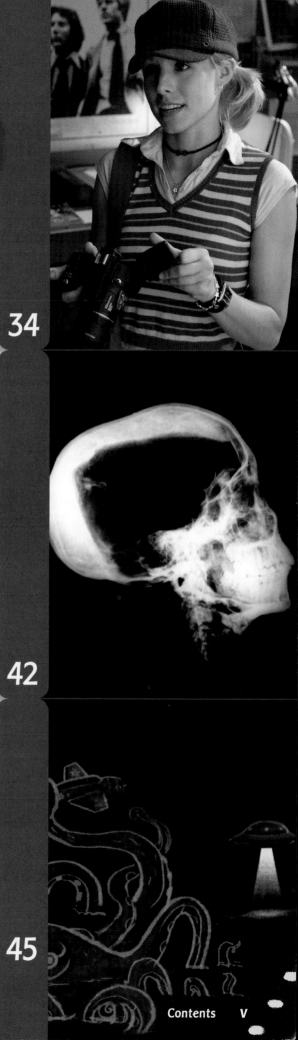

CONTENTS

Unit 4 — Fears and Phobias

93

105

109

Welcome to
Nelson Literacy

Nelson Literacy presents a rich variety of literature, informational articles, and media texts from Canada and around the world. Many of the selections offer tips to help you develop strategies in reading, oral communication, writing, and media literacy.

Here are the different kinds of pages you will see in this book:

Focus pages

These pages outline a specific strategy and describe how to use it. Included are "Transfer Your Learning" tips that show how you can apply that strategy to other strands and subjects.

Understanding Strategies

These selections have instructions in the margins that help you to understand and use reading, writing, listening, speaking, and media literacy strategies.

Applying Strategies

These selections give you the chance to apply the strategies you have learned. You will see a variety of formats and topics.

Transfer Your Learning

At the end of the unit, you'll have a chance to see how the strategies you have learned can help you in other subject areas such as Science and Technology, Geography, History, Health, Mathematics, and the Arts.

Mysteries

Can every mystery be solved?

Unit Learning Goals

- make inferences while reading
- write with a strong voice

- make inferences while listening
- create photo essays

- analyze generalization text pattern

Transfer Your Learning: Science and Technology

How to **Make Inferences**

When you make inferences you increase your understanding by making judgments, drawing conclusions, and reasoning about a text. You come up with *your own* ideas (about people, information, events, or situations in the text) by reading between the lines. These ideas are not stated explicitly.

You need to look for clues in the text and think about what you already know. Then put those clues and connections together to make inferences.

Do: Think about what you already know about the topic. → **Infer:** Make inferences about the theme or main idea of the selection.

Do: Look for clues that help you understand the people in the text (characters in fiction or real people in nonfiction texts). → **Infer:** Make inferences about their moods, attitudes, motivations, or personalities.

Do: Look for clues that tell you how people are responding to events. Make connections to how you would respond in a similar situation. → **Infer:** Make inferences about what is going on or how people feel about what is going on.

Confirm, change, or disregard inferences as you read on. Ask yourself: What do I think the author is *really* trying to tell me? What feelings or thoughts might be influencing my inferences?

Transfer Your Learning

Across the Strands

Writing: Good writers know that readers will make inferences, so they don't tell their readers everything. How could you improve a story you've written by allowing your readers to make inferences?

Across the Curriculum

Science: If you read the heading "Wasting Heat" in a science text you could use your prior knowledge to make an inference: wasting heat is bad and we should stop it. What inference do you make when you read the heading "Heat Pollution"?

Making Inferences

Think about what you already know and make inferences to figure out what the selection is about. How do the title and police tape help you make an inference about this story?

Talk About It

What do you think are the most important skills needed by those who solve crimes?

THE Killer's TALL TALE

Mystery Story by Jeremy Brown

Burton and Trellis walked toward the front door of the one-storey house. Detective Erin Radley was waiting for them on the overgrown concrete that led to the entrance.

"Morning, guys," Radley said.

"Mmm," said Burton.

"The boss hasn't had any coffee yet," Trellis said, "so I'll interpret. He said, 'And a good morning to you as well, Detective. You're looking quite nice today.'"

"Why, thank you, Wes," Radley said, looking at Trellis. "Wait a minute." She stepped next to the technician and squinted at his head. "Are you getting taller?"

Making Inferences →

Look for clues that help you understand the characters. What inferences can you make about Radley? What clues in the text help you make these inferences?

"Nah," Trellis said. "It's these new boots. They make me a few centimetres taller. And they give me more sole. Get it? Sole, soul?"

"Mmm," Burton said again.

"Do you feel that extra height equals extra authority?" Radley said. The extra height in Trellis's boots made him almost as tall as Radley, who stood 200 centimetres tall.

"Uh-oh," said Burton. He could almost see her taking out her mental notepad, collecting information for her book.

"Um, no, I just like the boots," Trellis said.

"I see," said Radley, nodding.

"Is that a bad answer?" Trellis asked, getting worried.

"I guess that depends," Radley said.

"I'm taking these boots back," said Trellis.

"Can we solve this crime first?" Burton said.

"I don't feel qualified to answer that," Trellis said. "These boots have ruined everything."

Radley smiled. Mike Trellis was always a good warm-up for interviewing suspects. "I'll give you the details before we go inside," she said. "The victim is Ellen Underwood, killed sometime last night. I have two suspects, Jim Danielson and Larry Saunders, who were both seen here with Underwood last night."

"Seen by whom?" Burton said.

"Each other," Radley said, cocking an eyebrow. "Danielson says he left first, so Saunders must have killed her. Saunders says he was the first one to leave and that Danielson must have done it. I know what you're going to say. Something about eyewitness accounts having glasses, not shoes, so they won't stand up in court."

"That's not bad," Burton said.

"Both guys are down at the station right now," said Radley. "I don't see either one of them changing his story, so we're going to need some hard evidence to get the killer to confess."

"Let's go see if the killer was nice enough to leave any evidence," Burton said and walked inside. "Mike, start taking video of the house, I'll handle the photos. We don't know how big the crime scene is yet, so let's get everything on film." They worked from room to room, eventually arriving at the doorway to the kitchen. Ellen Underwood's body was on the floor.

"Looks like she was killed in here," Burton said, still standing outside the doorway. He indicated the blood on the floor and cupboards. "She wasn't murdered somewhere else and moved to this room."

"I tried to get the killer to trip up," Radley said, "and mention something about the kitchen without me asking. But neither one did, so I had to come out and ask if they had been in this room. They both say they never went in the kitchen."

← **Making Inferences**

Use clues (including the art) and your prior knowledge to draw conclusions or make judgments. What knowledge from TV crime shows helps you understand what is going on in this scene? What inferences can you make about the situation?

Make connections to people you know. Who does Trellis remind you of? What inferences can you make about Trellis based on making this connection?

"I like the kitchen," Trellis said, "that's usually where the cookies are." He stepped into the doorway to get video of the room, his head almost touching the top of the door frame.

"Freeze!" Burton said, and Trellis dropped to the floor. Burton and Radley both looked down at him. "Man," Burton said, "that's the worst freeze I have ever seen."

"I thought you saw someone else in the house," Trellis said, still facedown on the floor. "I just wanted to clear your field of fire, in case you had to shoot."

"Always thinking," Burton said. He stepped over the technician.

"What do you see?" said Radley.

"I see a brown hair," said Burton, taking several photos of the strand, which was stuck to the wood trim above the doorway. "It's about an inch long and probably stuck to the wood with hair gel or wax." He took an evidence bag out of vest pocket 9 and a set of tweezers out of 24, plucked the hair off the frame, and sealed it in the bag.

"Both Danielson and Saunders have short brown hair," Radley said. "And I don't think we have enough probable cause to get DNA samples from either of them for comparison."

"How tall are they?" Burton said.

Radley thought about it. "Danielson is probably around 180 centimetres or so. Saunders is a little taller than me, so I'll put him at 205 centimetres."

"That's enough information for me," Burton said. "Tell Saunders we can prove he was in the room where Underwood was killed."

How did Burton know?

Burton's File

When Trellis walked into the kitchen doorway, his head almost touched the top of the frame. With his new boots, he stood about 200 centimetres, which makes the door frame a little higher than that. Saunders, at 205 centimetres, is the only suspect who would have been tall enough to brush his head against the frame and leave a hair sample behind.

Making Inferences

Look for clues that tell you how people are responding to events. Make connections to how you would respond. Put that information together to make an inference. What inferences can you make to help you figure out the solution?

Making Inferences

A graphic organizer like this can help you to organize your inferences.

Clues From the Text	+ Prior Knowledge	= Inference

Reflecting

Making Inferences: As you read the story, what inferences did you confirm? What inferences did you change or disregard? What personal thoughts or feelings might have influenced the inferences you made?

Metacognition: How does your background knowledge of crime investigation help you make reasonable inferences when reading mysteries?

Critical Thinking: What information does the author include to help you solve this mystery?

Talk About It
Why do brothers and sisters sometimes keep secrets
from each other?

The Buried Marbles Mystery

Novel Excerpt from *Cat's Eye* by Margaret Atwood

*Cat's Eye was written by Margaret Atwood, a popular Canadian author.
In this novel, Elaine, the main character, recalls her childhood during
the 1940s and 50s and the events that had a great impact on her life.*

One day someone appears in the schoolyard with a bag of
marbles, and the next day everyone has them. The boys desert
the boys' playground and throng into the common playground
in front of the BOYS and GIRLS doors; they need to come
to this side of the playground, because marbles have to be
played on a smooth surface and the boys' yard is all cinders.

For marbles you're either the person setting up the target
or the person shooting. To shoot you kneel down, sight, and
roll your marble at the target marble like a bowling ball.
If you hit it you keep it, and your own marble too. If you
miss, you lose your marble. If you're setting up, you sit on
the cement with your legs spread open and put a marble
on a crack in front of you. It can be an ordinary marble,
but these don't get many shooters, unless you offer two
for one. Usually the targets are more valuable: cat's
eyes, clear glass with a bloom of coloured petals in
the centre, red or yellow or green or blue; puries,
flawless like coloured water or sapphires or rubies;
waterbabies, with undersea filaments of colour
suspended in them; metal bowlies; aggies, like marbles
only bigger. These exotics are passed from winner to
winner. It's cheating to buy them; they have to be won.

Those with target marbles call out the names of their wares: *purie, purie, bowlie, bowlie*, the two-syllable words drawn out into a singsong, the voice descending, the way you call dogs, or children when they're lost. These cries are mournful, although they aren't meant to be. I sit that way myself, the cold marbles rolling in between my legs, gathering in my outspread skirt, calling out *cat's eye, cat's eye*, in a regretful tone, feeling nothing but avarice and a pleasurable horror.

The cat's eyes are my favourites. If I win a new one I wait until I'm by myself, then take it out and examine it, turning it over and over in the light. The cat's eyes really are like eyes, but not the eyes of cats. They're the eyes of something that isn't known but exists anyway; like the green eye of the radio; like the eyes of aliens from a distant planet. My favourite one is blue. I put it into my red plastic purse to keep it safe. I risk my other cat's eyes to be shot at, but not this one.

I don't collect many marbles because I'm not a very good shot. My brother is deadly. He takes five common marbles to school with him in a blue Crown Royal Whisky bag and comes back with the bag and his pockets bulging. He keeps his winnings in the screw–top Crown preserving jars, donated by my mother, which he lines up on his desk. He never talks about his skill though. He just lines up the jars.

One Saturday afternoon he puts all his best marbles—his puries, his waterbabies and cat's eyes, his gems and wonders—into a single jar. He takes it down into the ravine somewhere, in under the wooden bridge, and buries it. Then he makes an elaborate treasure map of where it's buried, puts it in another jar, and buries that one too. He tells me he's done these things but he doesn't say why, or where the jars are buried.

Reflecting

Making Inferences: What inferences did you make about the characters in this selection? What inferences did you make about why Elaine's brother buried the marbles?

Metacognition: How did making connections or looking for clues help you make inferences? How did your inferences affect your understanding of the characters in this selection?

Critical Literacy: Which character do you connect with most strongly: Elaine or her brother? How do you think the author has influenced the connection you form?

Talk About It
Imagine what it would be like to be hunted and in hiding.

Higher Animals

Short Story by Jay Henderson

Skye's heart fluttered like a bird in a cage—a wild bird, only moments trapped. They were out to get her, no doubt about that, and they always seemed to get what they wanted.

"Just about got you covered, Skye," wheezed Kevin, nearly out of breath from the chase.

"Hurry. Get yourself out of sight, too," Skye coaxed. She was amazed that Kevin had stuck with her, knowing how dangerous it had become. He was being uncommonly brave, offering to cover her first and then look after himself. She felt him toss a few last handfuls of poplar leaves over top of her. Then he made rustling noises burrowing into a separate pile they had prepared together. Skye inhaled the musky smell of decaying leaves, her nose pressed sideways against the cold and spongy forest floor. She prayed their tormentors would pass without detecting her red hair through the kaleidoscope of autumn colours. Otherwise she would end up dead and decaying too, if she weren't hidden well enough.

Neither said a word from then on. Everything was so quiet and still, Skye allowed herself the luxury of thinking that she and Kevin might have outsmarted their pursuers. Unfortunately, that possibility rapidly dissolved as the howls of the Hasher twins once again rang through the chill air.

It was clear that the twins had come over the ridge and were bearing down upon the hiding spot. One of them came crashing thought the bush nearby, sending shock waves into the earth. The side of Skye's face tingled as it picked up the vibrations. Was it Katie or Marla? Strange that one of them was running ahead of the other. The Hasher twins were weird; fourteen years old and still as inseparable as honey on toast.

Whoever had run ahead was getting closer. Closer and closer. "We're gonna eat you two for breakfast!" she screamed. It had to be Katie, Skye thought, judging by the raspy voice.

"Pack rats!" added Marla, catching up. Her yelp was unmistakable.

"Come on, you silly squirrels, show your faces!" bellowed a third voice: a boy's.

Oh no, not that new guy! worried Skye. Not fair; not fair at all. We're dead meat! We might have had a chance against the twins, but from what I've heard, this—what's his name—Todd, is an animal. They say he loves to see fear in his victim's eyes before he does them in.

Skye believed her heart would soon give her away. It was thump-thumping against her rib cage. One of them is bound to run right over us, she thought; there'll be a scream, and we'll be at their mercy. I know what they're like. I've seen Katie and Marla operate back at school. They never show sympathy for anybody smaller or weaker than themselves.

Rustling sounds. Someone was almost on top of her! Then a *craaack*! right next to Skye's head. The sound shot into her ear, but she remained frozen. She hoped Kevin was staying still, holding his breath also.

All fell silent. Her heart, starved for oxygen, slowed to the point where she was afraid it might stop breathing altogether. The world seemed locked in a freeze-frame. Skye expected an arm to thrust through the leaves any second and grab her by the neck. But it wasn't a hand she felt.

Something warm was making its way up her pant leg, rubbing its hairy body against the inside of her calf. It scurried a few centimetres, stopped, scurried and stopped, scurried and stopped. Gross me out, it's a mouse! she panicked.

It reached her knee. God, how she wished she had worn tight-fitting pants; how she wanted to scream—jump up—shake her leg—tear off her baggy jeans—whatever it might take to get the stupid thing out of there! But Skye couldn't. No way! Her life was more important than some ratty rodent using her pant leg as a hiding hollow.

Skye was determined to remain frozen in place, no matter where the little intruder went next—almost—but she absolutely had to let the air out of her lungs. Pursing her lips, she let it out ever so slowly, until she began to grow faint. Then she drew it in again like sucking yogurt through a narrow straw. Nothing mattered but her breathing, certainly not a harmless mouse, she told herself with a shiver. But, she began to wonder, was her breathing controlled enough, or was Katie standing there glaring down at the mound of browns and yellows covering her, watching it rise and fall like a blacksmith's bellows? Surely the thin layer of leaves wouldn't be enough of a covering to save her from the three beasts of Redmond Junior High.

Then the mouse started creeping its way up her thigh, heading for higher ground.

"Which way do you think the pond scum went, you guys?" Katie whispered. The others were close, too. Real close.

"I dunno. When they slipped over the ridge, I thought they were headed toward this big pine…" said Todd. "But now I'm not so sure."

"You hear that?" squealed Marla. "I bet they're escaping to the river, like all vermin when they're up against it." There were rustling sounds in the distance. The three immediately struck off.

Thwick! Katie's foot clipped the heel of Skye's boot as she sped off.

Oh God, no! Skye thought, tensing from temple to heel. The muscles in her neck, back and legs ached like they were being pulled together by stretchable bands running through her body. Even the mouse, who had managed to scale her thigh, stopped stone still. Thankfully, the boots continued to pound the earth, and the vibrations were rapidly diminishing in force. She relaxed, imagining the ends of three taut elastic bands in her body slowly coming together at the centre.

Elastic. The mouse was almost up to her panty line—definitely going too far! But was it safe to jump up yet? Were they far enough away? It was obvious that Kevin hadn't made a move yet. Reminding herself how serious the consequences of discovery would be, Skye decided to stay put a little longer. But the mouse had better not cross the elastic. If it moved, she moved!

Skye forced her mind, once again, to refocus. She thought it so unfair. The others had two obvious advantages: their superior strength and greater speed, compounded by the fact that they were ganging up. She knew it wouldn't matter to the twins that she wanted nothing from them, found it impossible to hate them.

Then Skye remembered what had happened to her two friends, Tracy and Twig. They would never run away again. Katie and Marla got them good. Skye had stayed hidden, watching from a safe distance as the twins picked them off one after the other. There had been no choice but to hide—*no* choice but to hide.

Skye's mind reeled as the mouse darted across the elastic and shot halfway up her right cheek where it lay down, trembling. It tickled. Skye twitched her cheek. The mouse reacted quickly, making a break for it down the back of her leg and out the end of the pant tunnel, scratching her with its tiny claws all the way.

"Kevin. Kevin, let's move it!" Skye commanded. She leapt to her feet. Immediately hunching back down, she checked all around. "They're bound to backtrack and sniff us out if we stay put."

❧

"Oh this is great! They'll never find us here, not a chance. How'd you spot it?" Kevin asked, huddled against the wall of a small cave, high up on the riverbank.

"Caught a glimpse of it out the corner of my eye. Probably an old washout. Maybe a grizzly dug into it for a den." Skye sat close to the entrance, scanning what she could see of the riverbank.

"What!" blurted Kevin. " Grizzly?"

"Shhhhh! Keep it down." That waterfall up the way would cover some noises, but it was better to be safe. Even if he had shown some courage earlier, Kevin was still no Robin Hood. She was pleased to have his companionship, though.

"Sorry," he whispered. "But if some smelly old sack of a bear once used this as a home and comes back to claim it, we're gonna be nothing but lunch."

"Kevin, I think I hear something."

"It's the bear! It's hibernating time again and we're…"

"Shhh!" Skye scolded, whispering, "don't say another word."

They both sat absolutely still, once again holding their breaths. Sure enough, there were noises—and soon, voices.

"Look, there're fresh tracks here!" howled Todd.

"Yep, that's one of them all right," spoke Katie, sounding as always like someone had rubbed the inside of her voice-box with sandpaper.

"C'mon, c'mon, they gotta be hiding right around here somewhere," yelped Marla. "Let's find 'em and toast 'em!" Skye pictured Marla with a string of drool running out the corner of her crooked mouth. She would be hanging at Katie's shoulder.

"Not so fast," Katie said. "There are more tracks heading further upstream. See? They've gone up past the waterfall into the pines."

"I think you're right," replied Todd. "Let's go, you guys. We have to put those two away once and for all!" The sounds of their huffs and grunts quickly faded away.

Skye, letting the air out of her lungs and gasping for more, suddenly found herself wrapped up in Kevin's arms. He, too, was struggling to get his breathing back to normal, but obviously couldn't contain his joy at having dodged the grim reaper again. "Ha! What a bunch of idiots," he said, "they couldn't track an elephant across a field of chocolate pudding."

Then he laughed. Skye laughed, too. They laughed and hugged, and rocked and laughed and held each other tightly in the middle of the little cave, right where the grizzly had probably rested its massive head.

All of a sudden, a head appeared in the entranceway. "Ewwww, you two look pretty cozy." Reaching in, Katie grabbed Skye by the collar of her coat and plucked her out. Kevin stepped out peacefully, not looking anyone in the eye, his face flushed and turning redder by the second.

Katie faced Skye head on, staring her down. "Now then, I think you've got something I want!" Suddenly her right arm shot forward, toward Skye's middle. Twisting her fist around as she thrust it ahead, Katie opened it palm up and ordered, "Put it there."

Skye immediately reached for the metal loop attached to her belt. She only had one life tag left, and was certain that Katie knew it. Disconnecting the loop from her belt, she slid off the piece of leather with the word SQUIRREL stamped into it, and placed it in Katie's hand.

"You are officially dead meat!" squealed Marla. "I believe the graveyard is up that way." Drooling more than she normally did, Marla pointed toward the hill where the Animal Game had started over an hour ago.

"So sorry—aren't we girls?" said Todd, his eyes gleaming like those of a wolf ready for the kill. Yanking Kevin's last life tag from his belt, Todd took off in pursuit of two orange-shirted upper herbivores who were making a break for the pines. Katie and Marla struck off as well.

As Skye and Kevin trudged toward the Animal Graveyard to twiddle their thumbs until the end of the game, Kevin took hold of Skye's hand, saying, "Next time, let's ask to be carnivores or upper omnivores maybe. We could be the grizzlies."

"Higher animals, eh? Grizzlies could be all right, I guess," Skye mused, squeezing Kevin's hand tightly. A broad smile floated across her face before she added, "How's your bear hug, Kevin?"

Reflecting

Making Inferences: What inferences did you make about the characters as you read? What ideas or conclusions did your inferences help you form?

Metacognition: How does imagining how the characters feel engage you in the story?

Critical Thinking: What did you think the title "Higher Animals" meant when you began reading? What do you think the title means now?

Talk About It
Does being wise mean you have all of the answers?

The Hermit's Secret

Legend by Leslie J. Wyatt

Long before the Kingdom of Rillen became known for its silver trees, there lived a wise old hermit. He dwelled on the Mountain of Three Kings, close to where the Golden River bursts out of the rock and starts its journey to the sea. The old man passed his time quietly tending his animals and garden. Scarcely a day went by that someone did not make a pilgrimage to the humble man.

"Go see the wise man," was the advice people gave to those who were confused, troubled, grieving, or struggling. "Go. He will help."

A youth by the name of Alath lived at the foot of the mountain, on the Plain of Narra, where the silver trees would one day grow. He watched people start up the path to the hermit's house with troubled faces. He saw them come back at peace, helped and comforted. What happened on that mountain? Who was this old man who never came down except on the eve of Queen Maris's Day?

So one morning Alath decided to set out to see the wise old man. "Mother," he said as he shouldered his pack, "I will return when I know the hermit's secret."

The journey was not hard, for the path was well trodden. The second sun had just cleared the highest peak when Alath arrived at the old man's hut.

"Greetings, young traveller," the hermit said. His hair and beard were as white as the clouds that rested on the mountains. "What brings you to my humble house?"

"If you please, sir, I would like to learn the secret of how you help the travellers who seek your advice."

The man laughed. "You are not the first to so desire. I will say to you as I said to them—if you watch well, you will understand."

So Alath watched. Soon a pilgrim appeared.

"Oh, kind sir!" he said, shaking the hermit's hand. "Please help me. You must tell me what I should do. I have the chance to buy a field from a neighbour, but it will take every last minna I have. If my other crops do poorly this season, I could lose not only the new field, but my entire farm as well." The man wrung his hands.

"Mmmm. You might have a good opportunity there," said the hermit.

"Yes. Sort of. I mean—it's my family that wants the land. They think it's my great chance." The man sat down beside Alath and the old man. "Actually, I don't want any more land than I already have. It's as much as I can take care of now."

"Ah. I understand." The wise man's voice was soothing, like a drink of cool water on a hot summer day. He listened while the man shared his problem. After a while, the hermit asked Alath to fetch a honeymelon from the garden. As the three slurped their way through the golden fruit and chewed the sweet red seeds, the farmer talked on. He spoke of his farm and of his desire to live a simple life. Most of all, he spoke of the strangely beautiful seedling trees he had purchased from a stranger during the last Festival of New Harvest.

"You must see them someday, sir. Twelve of them, and silver as a newly minted coin," he said, his tired eyes lighting with excitement. "I spend much of my time taking care of them."

NEL

Alath kept wondering when the hermit would give the farmer the answer to his problem, but the old man only said, "Perhaps you have a greater treasure in your little trees than your family knows."

The man flushed. "That I couldn't say, sir, but I do know I am happiest while gazing on their shining leaves." He heaved another sigh. "Why should I want more land to take me away from them? Or cause me to lose them…." He fell silent then, his eyebrows moving up and down, now smiling, now frowning, as if carrying on a conversation in his mind. All the while, the old hermit said nothing. He just continued to gaze off over the mountain and eat the sweet red seeds.

When the farmer finished his melon, he rose to go. "I think you are right," he said. "I do not need the field and would be better off tending my silver trees. I do thank you very much."

Alath stared at the departing figure. Had the old hermit given some advice while he, Alath, had been fetching the melon? Somehow he didn't think so, since the farmer had still been talking about the same subject when Alath had returned as when he had left.

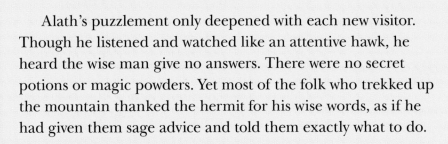

Alath's puzzlement only deepened with each new visitor. Though he listened and watched like an attentive hawk, he heard the wise man give no answers. There were no secret potions or magic powders. Yet most of the folk who trekked up the mountain thanked the hermit for his wise words, as if he had given them sage advice and told them exactly what to do.

Several months passed, but Alath felt no closer to discovering the hermit's secret. Each pilgrim's visit was much the same. After a warm welcome, the travellers poured out their problems. The old man listened intently, offering sympathy or letting them know he understood their problem.

Alath was sure he missed no part of the conversations, no motion of the hermit's hands. Still, by the time the visitors left, they usually offered many thanks for their host's wise counsel.

Perhaps I should return home, Alath thought in discouragement. I am no closer to learning the hermit's secret than when I first arrived. Yet he hated to give up. Then one foggy morning the old man became ill and had to stay in bed. As Alath brought him broth made from meadowfern, there came a knock on the door.

"Oh no!" exclaimed Alath. "Someone is here to see you. Shall I tell them to come back another day?"

The man smiled. "No. You go."

With his heart in his stomach, Alath greeted the newest pilgrim. "Hello, ma'am."

"Good morning, young man. I am here to see the wise man," she said as she handed him a loaf of fresh bread.

Alath took the gift and bowed low. "I am truly sorry, but he is sick today. Is there anything I can do to help?" How foolish, Alath thought, to be saying this to a woman more than three times my age.

The woman sighed and sank into a chair. "What answer could you give me? You are so young. You don't know how it is to have a son who wants to go off to the town to be a merchant and leave the farm he was to inherit," she sighed.

NEL

"How difficult that must be for you," Alath said, sorry that he had no words of wisdom for the troubled lady.

"Yes, difficult. I desperately need someone to take care of the farm." By now the woman was dabbing at tears with her handkerchief. "I don't know why, but my son has never loved the land. All he ever wants to do is buy and sell and make money."

"Mmmm," murmured Alath as he handed her a cup of mingberry tea, its multi-coloured steam swirling and rising like a miniature sunset.

She smiled a grateful smile. "Sometimes I think we'd both be better off if he became a merchant and hired a man to work the farm."

"It's hard to know what to do, isn't it?" Alath said. If only the hermit were here. He would help the poor woman. "Let me serve you some bread," he added, wanting only to run down the path and leave the hermit and his undiscovered secret far behind.

Alath cut two slices of the fragrant bread the woman had brought. Spreading them with thick, yellow butter, he hastened back to the woman, who stared at the hearth fire as if seeing something there.

"Here, your bread will strengthen you for your homeward journey," he said.

Together they sipped tea, munched the salty-sweet goodness of the bread, and talked of the latest news in the Kingdom of Rillen.

At length the woman stood. "Yes, I think my son would be very happy to be a merchant. He is certainly very unhappy on the farm, and I do want him to be happy. Perhaps if he became a merchant, we could sell the farm, and I could go live with him in the town…" Her voice trailed off to nothing, and she stood motionless for a long while.

Alath waited. What should he say? What a failure he had been with his first pilgrim. As soon as possible, he would head down the path to the valley and leave the hermit's secret for someone else to discover.

The lady turned to him. "Young man, thank you very much. I thought that I would receive no help because the wise man was not able to see me. But I must say that he has an able assistant. Perhaps my son and I will come someday and tell you how your solution worked."

She waved a farewell and started off down the mountain in the thinning fog. Alath stared after her for a long while before once more entering the hermit's hut.

Carrying another cup of mingberry tea and a slice of bread, he went to check on the old man. "Some food for you, sir?" he asked.

"Why, thank you, Alath," the hermit said. "Tell me how the visit went. Did you know the answers?"

"No. I knew no answers. I just listened."

"H'mmm…."

"No wise words," Alath said. "No great advice."

He stared at the small hearth fire as he thought of the woman's parting words, then turned to the old man and smiled. "But I'm wondering if sometimes listening isn't the best answer of all."

And so it was that as year followed year and pilgrims continued to trek up the mountain, word spread throughout the Kingdom of Rillen that the young man who lived with the hermit was as wise as his mentor.

Reflecting

Metacognition: What text-to-text or text-to-self connections did you make as you read this legend? How did making connections help you make inferences?

Critical Literacy: What stereotypes does this selection use? How could the selection be rewritten to avoid stereotypes? Why are you more likely to find stereotypes in legends and fairytales?

Connecting to Other Media: Think about how this legend could be adapted to appear in the following forms: picture book, movie, cartoon, or radio play. Which form do you think would be most effective? Why do you think so?

How to ➤ Write With a Strong Voice

When we speak our voices convey a range of emotions and we can sound sarcastic or sincere. Writing also has a voice. Voice in writing is how our words sound to the reader. Writing is more enjoyable and interesting to read when it has a strong voice—a personality. Create a strong writing voice by using

| friendly or formal tone | ● | word choice | ● | patterns of sentences |

> Compare the voice in these two writing samples. Which voice do you prefer? Why?
>
> One night, Snappy our pet snake got loose. We only found out about it when we heard our neighbour scream.
>
> ⬇
>
> It was a hot and silent night. A bloodcurdling scream split the air. Loud grating noises came from the alley between the dark houses, as if bricks were being thrown down a metal slide. From an open window came the sudden cry of "Snappy!" The snake was loose again.

Match tone to purpose.

Before you write, think about your purpose and what tone is most appropriate. For example, an informal tone is fine when you're writing a note to friends about your weekend, but it's not appropriate if you're writing a cover letter for a job.

Match word choice and sentence structure to audience.

A long, formal, serious report about treasure hunting is fine for an audience of archaeologists, but a short, simple, friendly article would be better for an audience of young students. Choose appropriate words and sentence structures for your audience.

Know your topic.

A writer who knows the subject matter well is able to write with confidence. If you're writing with a strong voice, it usually means you know your topic well and are enthusiastic about it.

Transfer Your Learning

Across the Strands

Media Literacy: Movies could also be described as having a voice: serious or funny, realistic or fantastic, and so on. Describe the voice of a movie you've seen recently. What contributes to this voice?

Across the Curriculum

History: How important do you think it is for a history selection to have a strong voice?

Talk About It

If you had to hide something valuable, what would you do to make sure no one else would ever find it?

The Mystery of Oak Island

Nonfiction Article by Mark Reynolds

Daniel McGinnis could barely contain his excitement as he led his friends John Smith and Anthony Vaughn through the wooded shade of Oak Island in Nova Scotia in the early summer of 1795.

Daniel had been exploring the island just the day before. Now his two friends followed him through the trees of the near empty island to a small clearing on the southeastern end. When they arrived at the clearing they could see an oak tree, one of the many from which the island took its name. Hanging from a forked branch was an old tackle block from a ship.

The clearing was human-made. The three young men could see numerous tree stumps and remnants of trees cut some years before. But tree stumps were not what interested the boys right then. The cause of Daniel's excitement was a 30 cm pit in the ground under the dangling ship's tackle. Though it was grown over with vegetation, the boys could tell that whatever had caused this irregularity was not natural. They knew right away that whatever they had found, it had to be important.

Steeped in the pirate lore of the island, the boys were certain that all that stood between them and a life of leisure was a few hours of digging. The many inlets and harbours of Oak Island had made ideal hiding places for pirate ships in the past. Pirates were notorious for hiding their treasure so no one could ever find it. And if it were pirate treasure, why not the legendary treasure of Captain Kidd?

The pit was evidently an old shaft that had been filled in. But after digging a few metres, the boys found only platforms of oak logs embedded in the sides of the shaft. That proved to them that something had been buried there. But they didn't have the tools to continue and had to abandon their quest.

These boys were the first to dig at Oak Island. But they weren't the last. The next time someone tried to find the treasure, the cavity filled with seawater. That continued to happen every time another attempt was made. Whoever had constructed the shaft had set a trap—dig to a certain depth and flood tunnels connected to the bay would fill the tunnel with water.

There followed over 200 years of fruitless attempts to find the Oak Island Treasure. The pit became known as the Money Pit—as much for the money that treasure hunters spent trying to find treasure as for the money rumoured to be buried in the pit. Each new searcher had a new plan of how to recover the treasure. Each met with failure.

The latest treasure hunters need $15 million to make their plan work. They are confident that with modern technology and careful study, they will succeed where so many have failed. Maybe they will.

How much treasure is down there? Is there a treasure? Will new technology ever solve the mystery? For now, the Money Pit yields only more questions. There are all kinds of theories about who buried the treasure on Oak Island.

- **Captain Kidd**, the famous pirate, buried treasure on Oak Island. In fact, one of Kidd's maps points to Oak Island.

- **Sir Francis Bacon**, rumoured to be the real author of Shakespeare's plays, buried the original "Shakespeare" manuscripts on Oak Island.

- **The Incas of Peru,** after being conquered by the Spanish, buried their gold and silver on Oak Island.

- **Natural causes** — the so-called Money Pit is a natural *sinkhole* (ground that has settled over a space in the rock below). Naturally formed underground caverns are common in the island's bedrock.

Reflecting

Reading Like a Writer: How would you describe the voice this author uses? Do you think his voice is appropriate for his purpose and audience? Explain.

Metacognition: How did analyzing tone, word choice, and sentence structure clarify your understanding of voice in this article?

Critical Thinking: Given the information, and your background knowledge, which of the four theories of who buried the treasure seems most likely?

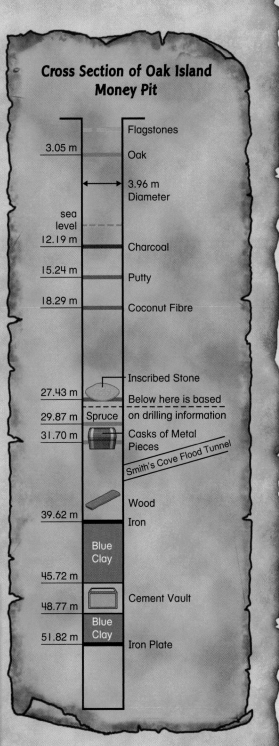

Cross Section of Oak Island Money Pit

3.05 m	Flagstones / Oak
	3.96 m Diameter
sea level 12.19 m	Charcoal
15.24 m	Putty
18.29 m	Coconut Fibre
27.43 m	Inscribed Stone — Below here is based
29.87 m	Spruce / on drilling information
31.70 m	Casks of Metal Pieces
	Smith's Cove Flood Tunnel
39.62 m	Wood / Iron
	Blue Clay
45.72 m	
48.77 m	Cement Vault
51.82 m	Blue Clay / Iron Plate

This diagram shows what has happened at the Money Pit over the last 200 years.

Talk About It
What do you know about the mystery of the Aurora Borealis, also known as the Northern Lights?

INVESTIGATING THE
Aurora Borealis

**Radio Transcript by Patricia Bell
from CBC Radio**

Patricia Bell: Scientists have been studying the Aurora Borealis for decades, but they still don't know where and when the Northern Lights will paint the sky with shades of red, green, and purple, or what causes the patterns and swirls. They hope to get some answers by putting up sixteen observatories with automated cameras across Canada's north over the next year. Dr. Eric Donavan is with the University of Calgary.

Eric Donovan: You will see why Canada has historically been so very important in studies of the Aurora, because if you look at that Aurora oval, Canada occupies the bulk of the land mass under the Aurora oval.

Patricia Bell: Many admire the stunning beauty of the Northern Lights, but they can spell trouble. Auroral storms can cause electrical outages, and interfere with radio communications and global positioning systems. That causes havoc for both civilians and the military. That's why scientists want to understand just how they work. Mary Ellen Thomas is executive director of the Nunavut Research Institute. She says the project will do more than just answer scientific questions.

Mary Ellen Thomas: Well, it's great when you can learn something that's in your own backyard, and making science interesting to kids is good for education.

Patricia Bell: In October 2006, scientists sent five satellites into space in a special orbit for two years. Together with the cameras on the ground, they will be able to capture the Aurora Borealis from all angles and, hopefully, understand where and when the greatest light show of all will take place.

WHAT ARE THE NORTHERN LIGHTS?

Inuit storyteller Michael Kusugak explains what his people believe about the Northern Lights.

We believe when you die, your soul goes up into the heavens. And on a clear moonlit night, all those people up there like to go out. And what they like to do is they like to play soccer, and that is what the northern lights are—the trails of the souls of the dead playing soccer in the sky.

Their scientific name is *Aurora Borealis*. We call them "Aqsalijaat: the trail of those playing soccer." On Baffin Island, they are known simply as "Aqsarniit: Soccer Trails." They like to come out when the sky is crisp and clear and the stars are twinkling brightly in the heavens. Sometimes they are a milky white colour, sometimes they are all the colours of the rainbow.

Soccer is a traditional game of the Inuit. In early winter, the sea ice becomes a giant playing field, flat and smooth. Since the days become shorter and shorter as you move farther north in winter, we like to play at night when the stars are out and the moon is bright. It is our belief that the souls of the dead also like to indulge in the lively game of soccer as they did when they were living. They run all over the sky chasing a walrus head that they use for a soccer ball. And that is what the Northern Lights are.

Our loved ones die; my grandparents died when I was a little boy, my father died in 1973. It is a great consolation to go out on a clear moonlit night and watch them enjoy a game of soccer.

Reflecting

Reading Like a Writer: Compare the voices in the two pieces on pages 26 and 27. Considering the voice, which audience is the radio transcript most suitable for? Why? Which audience is Michael Kusugak's piece most suitable for? Why?

Metacognition: Do you find it easier to think about voice when you read two very different selections or when you read instructions about improving voice? How does comparing the use of voice in these two pieces help you understand the writing trait voice?

Critical Literacy: Each piece offers a different perspective about the Northern Lights. Why is it important to read about each perspective?

Talk About It

What makes a person want to risk his/her life to do something that has never been done before?

AMELIA EARHART

Poems by Monica Kulling

Amelia Earhart was the first woman to fly solo across the Atlantic. In 1937, she and her navigator disappeared in the middle of her attempt to fly solo around the world. What happened remains a mystery to this day. In the following poem Amelia is the speaker— the poem is told from her point of view. Canadian poet Monica Kulling has long been fascinated by Amelia's life and disappearance.

May 20, 1932

MISS EARHART
BREAKS RECORD

STORMING

planes began for me
at an air show
I watched
a little red plane
storming stunts
in the wide sky
figure eights
barrel-rolls
looping-the-loops
the little red plane
tore up the sky
then dove straight at me
but I didn't move a hair
I stared that plane down
it pulled back
in the nick of time
roaring over my head:
"I dare you!"

more than anything
that made me want to fly
that made me decide

Earhart first again

Earhart crosses Atlantic

AmeliaCramped

inthe
cockpit
likeabirdinabox
theicecakedwings   theicecakedwings
shebringsjuice
toothbrush&comb
couragethewill
tofly15hrs
without
stop
throughdarkdanger
the
Atlantic
night

Earhart missing

Reflecting

Reading Like a Writer: A poem written from the point of view of a person should capture the voice of that person. What can you tell about Amelia by thinking about the voice in "Storming"?

Making Inferences: As you read "Storming," what inferences do you make about Amelia? How does the background information help you make inferences?

Metacognition: How does thinking about voice help you make inferences?

How to

Make Inferences While Listening

Have you ever had a conversation in which someone got really angry but you thought they were just fooling around? If so, you know how important it is to make inferences while listening. Usually, there is a lot more going on when someone speaks than just what you can hear (or see in the speaker's expressions, posture, or gestures). You need to make inferences by putting together all the clues in the text with what you already know.

- Use your prior knowledge of the speaker and topic to help you make inferences.

- Think about the speaker's tone and what his/her expressions, posture, or gestures tell you about that tone. Ask yourself: What emotion can I identify in his/her voice? What does that tell me about the speaker's mood or about the meaning of the text?

- Use clues, like the speaker's tone or word choice, to identify the implicit message.

- As you listen, think about the inferences you've made. Confirm, change, or disregard inferences as you get more information.

Experiment by asking someone to say "Will your parents be home?" in a variety of ways using different gestures and expressions. For example,

- As the parent of a friend asking the question before allowing your friend to come to your house

- As the friend, hoping your parents will be home

- As the friend, hoping your parents will not be home

Transfer Your Learning

Across the Strands

Media: You also need to make inferences as you listen to media texts (news or songs on the radio, TV shows, or movies). What do you think might make that task harder? What might make it easier?

Across the Curriculum

History: In history class, you sometimes listen to important speeches or debates. Why do you think it's important to make inferences while listening to this type of text?

Talk About It

Why do you think a place might be called *Head-Smashed-In Buffalo Jump*?

Welcome to Head-Smashed-In Buffalo Jump

Virtual Tour from the Head-Smashed-In Buffalo Jump Interpretive Centre

Open on scene of prairie and tourist interpretive centre. Camera pans 360 degrees to show view of prairie as narrator speaks, slowly, calmly, and clearly.

Narrator (Voice-over): Here, at the natural sandstone escarpment called the Porcupine Hills Formation of southern Alberta, Canada, is where the prairie begins.

Step back in time thousands of years to understand an important human activity, unique to the western plains.

Making Inferences

Use your prior knowledge and new information to make an inference. What human activity happened at Head-Smashed-In Buffalo Jump? What clues support your inference?

This is where all the elements of earth and sky, wind, sun, and topography combined to offer the perfect conditions for organized communal bison drives.

Making Inferences →

Confirm, change, or disregard inferences as you get more information. Can you confirm your earlier inference about human activity? If not, how does your inference change?

Walk the trails where archaeologists have found over 6000 years of bones and artifacts, that have earned this place a United Nations "World Heritage Site" designation.

Making Inferences →

Use clues, like word choice, to make inferences about the implicit messages. The explicit message is that this place has earned a "World Heritage Site" designation. The implicit message is that this is an important, historical site.

Explore seven levels of displays and multimedia presentations in a one-of-a-kind visitor centre, built right into the face of the cliff.

The Alberta Government, in consultation with the Piikani and Kainai bands of the Blackfoot Confederacy First Nations, maintains the stewardship of this special place.

Learn about Napi and how he helped the Creator bring this world and its creatures into existence. Learn about Napi's people and the buffalo culture that flourished for thousands of years.

Guided tours and special events are offered year round. In summer you might find yourself sleeping in our tipi camp or moving to the beat of Blackfoot drums at our weekly dance performances.

Head-Smashed-In Buffalo Jump: come hear our stories and experience the days of the buffalo.

Making Inferences

Think about the speaker's tone. How do you think this speaker sounds as he's giving this virtual tour? Serious or humorous? What makes you think so?

Reflecting

Making Inferences: What inferences about Head-Smashed-In Buffalo Jump did you make?

Metacognition: Do you find it easier to make inferences while you're listening or while you're reading? What does that say about how you learn?

Critical Literacy: Identify the purpose and point of view in this media text. Who might have a different point of view about this topic?

APPLYING
LISTENING
STRATEGIES

▶ Making Inferences

Talk About It
What do you expect a TV show detective to be like?

Veronica
MARS
Life's tough. She's tougher.

Rant by Ananda Fulton

Mix equal parts courage, compassion, brains, and sass and you get Veronica Mars—my personal hero and the main character of a TV show that rocked prime time with witty dialogue and compelling characters. I don't understand why the show was cancelled after only three seasons. I loved watching Veronica track down dog-snatchers and murderers—she was clever, tech-savvy, and passionate about justice.

The network never should have cancelled such a smart and stylish show. After all, we don't see enough true female heroes on TV or elsewhere in the media: girls and women who, like Veronica, are strong-minded and independent, brilliant and self-assured, brave and just. Veronica was even more likable and realistic a character because she was far from perfect. She sometimes jumped to the wrong conclusions, she didn't always get the criminal, and she often needed a little help from her friends to outsmart the bad guys.

In addition to giving us such a classy young hero, the show balanced a complex series of mysteries. Some mysteries were solved within one episode and some spanned multiple seasons. The characters weren't always what they seemed to be and the plotlines were sprinkled with comedy, tragedy, loyalty, and revenge. It was encouraging to see a show that believed its teen audience was smart enough to appreciate these storylines. I think TV networks should fight harder to keep such thought-provoking shows on the air. Don't you agree that we need more heroes like Veronica Mars?

As Veronica would say, "Tragedy blows through your life like a tornado, uprooting everything. Creating chaos. You wait for the dust to settle and then you choose. You can live in the wreckage and pretend it's still the mansion you remember. Or you can crawl from the rubble and slowly rebuild."

Cancelled! Wouldn't you have wanted the opportunity to get to know this super-clever detective better?

Veronica: You must be Kizza.

Kizza: Yes, uh, I'm looking for Detective Mars.

Veronica: I'm Detective Mars.

Kizza: You're just a girl. You're a—you're a teenager.

Veronica: A girl, a teenager, and a private detective. I'm a triple threat. Barely fits on my business card.

Reflecting

Making Inferences: From her rant, what inferences can you make about this author? If you were listening to this rant on the radio, what tone would you expect the author to use?

Metacognition: Are you able to understand this selection, even if you haven't watched an episode of *Veronica Mars*? What does the author do to help you understand the show and her viewpoint?

Connecting to Other Media: Compare or contrast TV show detectives you know with Veronica Mars and what you know about her. Would you consider Veronica a stereotypical detective? A stereotypical teenager?

NEL

Veronica Mars. Life's tough. She's tougher. 35

How to

Create a Photo Essay

Photo essays use photos and captions to tell a story or highlight a theme. Because the photos often personalize the material, photo essays allow viewers to more easily connect with the story or theme.

Steps in Creating a Photo Essay

1. Think about what you want your photo essay to do: tell a story or highlight a theme. For example, your theme could be "The World's Biggest Mysteries."

2. Gather a dozen photos that reflect your theme or story. For example, photos of Big Foot or the Loch Ness Monster would be perfect for "The World's Biggest Mysteries." (It just might be hard for you to find *real* photos!)

3. Spread your photos out. Decide which ones you're going to use, or if you need more.

4. Decide what order the photos should be presented in— sequentially, randomly, or some other way. For example, from the photo with the most impact to the one with the least. Your theme or story may influence your organization.

5. The colour and content of the photos may also influence organization. Experiment with where the photos are placed. Overlap some photos, place others on an angle, allow some photos to take up a whole page, or crowd lots of photos on a page—whatever works best.

6. Write brief captions that highlight your theme and help the photos tell your story. Experiment with fonts, sizes, and colours.

7. Have someone else view your photo essay. Ask: "Do you understand my theme or the story I'm trying to tell? How do the photos make you feel?" Make revisions and create a final draft of your photo essay.

Surrounded by Mystery

Photo Essay by Kristiina Paul

Is that a blossom? A bug? A reptile? What secrets does the camera capture?

Transfer Your Learning

Across the Strands

Writing: What did you learn in this unit about improving voice that might be useful as you create a photo essay?

Across the Curriculum

History: History can be brought to life in a photo essay. What photos would you use to depict a theme of conflict?

Talk About It

What does it take to be a great detective?

Detecting
Women
Onscreen

Photo Essay by Michelle Lee

How often do you think of women when you hear the word *detective*? Women detectives in movies and TV shows have really changed over the years. Women have gone from spunky sidekicks to competent professionals. Gentle old ladies who solve crimes in their spare time have been replaced by powerful forensic scientists and police detectives.

Creating a Photo Essay →

Photo essays use photos and captions to tell a story or highlight a theme. What does this title reveal about the theme of the photo essay?

1946, Vivian Sternwood in *The Big Sleep* helps the hardboiled private eye.

1934, Nora Charles in *The Thin Man* is half of a witty couple who solve crimes.

NEL

1965 to 1969, Emma Peel in
The Avengers is a cool amateur.

← Creating a Photo Essay

To create a photo essay, you need lots of photos connected to your theme or story. Do you think this photo essay needs more or fewer photos? What other photos would you want to see? What would you have left out?

1968 to 1972, Julie Barnes in *The Mod Squad* is a hip undercover officer.

← Creating a Photo Essay

To create a photo essay, you need to decide on your organizational structure. Some photo essays follow a sequential pattern. Does the theme of female detectives need to be presented sequentially? How else could it be presented?

1976 to 1981, the three private detectives in *Charlie's Angels* work for Charlie.

Experiment with where photos are placed. Does the placement of photos in this photo essay work? What would you change?

1982 to 1988, *Cagney and Lacey* are the first female police team on TV.

1982 to 1987, Laura Holt in *Remington Steele* invents a male boss so clients will hire her.

1993 to 2002, Dana Scully in *The X Files* is a logical, calm investigator.

Anita Van Buren in *Law & Order* is a tough chief.

Creating a Photo Essay

A photo essay includes brief captions that highlight the theme or help tell the story. What other information would you like to see in these captions?

Catherine Willows in *CSI* is a blood spatter analyst.

Mary Spalding in *Intelligence* is the director of a spy agency.

Monica Rawlings is a police captain on *The Shield*.

← **Creating a Photo Essay**

The last step in creating a photo essay is checking that it successfully tells the story or highlights the theme. Now that you've viewed all of this photo essay, what do you think its theme is? What story does it tell?

Reflecting

Creating Photo Essays: How effectively does this photo essay tell its story or reveal its theme?

Metacognition: How does viewing a photo essay help you understand how to create one? What else do you need to help you understand how to create a photo essay?

Connecting to Other Media: Think about detectives you know from watching TV shows or movies, or reading books. What characteristics do these detectives have in common? How are detectives stereotyped? What aspect of the stereotype do you think is most true? Least true?

Talk About It
Can modern forensics solve a mystery over 3000 years old?

KING TUT'S
MYSTERIOUS DEATH

Photo Essay by Kristin Baird Rattini

Egypt's most famous king—King Tutankhamen—died at age 19. The puzzle has fascinated researchers since 1922. Determined to find the answer, National Geographic Explorer-in-Residence Zahi Hawass used modern technology to find out why.

Inside Tut's burial chamber, Zahi Hawass is face to face with the mummy.

An old X-ray from 1968 showed a bone fragment loose in the mummy's skull. Many investigators suspected Tut had been fatally hit from behind. The CT scans show the skull was broken after Tut's death.

Forensic artists recreated the young king's face using skull measurements from digital images of the mummy.

King Tut's mummy slides into the CT scanning machine. Scans give information about breaks in bones and other injuries. Scans of the mummy show no evidence of any long term illness or poison.

Could an adviser (called Aye) have killed the king to gain power for himself? This painting shows Aye (right) with King Tut.

New digital images (like this one) of Tut's mummy provide clues to how the king died.

Fracture

Did this injury kill Tut? The CT scans reveal that King Tut broke his leg shortly before his death. This injury could have led to a fatal infection, but we may never know for sure that it caused his death.

Even with the best high-tech tools, it looks like the case of King Tut may never be completely solved.

Reflecting

Analyzing Photo Essays: In your opinion, does this photo essay tell a story effectively? What elements of the photo essay do you find most effective? What would you have done differently?

Metacognition: Which would you prefer reading: a photo essay, a magazine article, or a story about mummies? Why? In your response, think about the amount of information in each type of text and how that information is conveyed.

Generalization

Here's one example of an outline for an essay using this pattern.

Generalization—Grade 7 students should do an hour of homework every night.

↓

Support—Homework has been proven to result in better marks on end-of-unit tests.

↓

Support—Completing homework every night helps students develop good work habits, something they will need throughout their lives.

↓

Opposing Argument— Students already have too much to do outside of school.

Generalization text pattern can be used for essays, speeches, newspaper editorials, or nonfiction articles. A generalization text pattern organizes information into a general statement followed by facts, reasons, or examples that are intended to support it.

This pattern is often used to present an argument. Sometimes the writer will include opposing points as well as supporting points, providing arguments against the opposing points that support his/her argument or theory.

Using generalization text pattern can help your readers follow your argument. Likewise, if you're reading a text with this pattern, understanding the pattern will help you understand and remember what you read.

You can identify generalization text pattern by looking for words and phrases such as *theory*, *as a result*, *one reason*, *therefore*, *in conclusion*, *because*, *argument*.

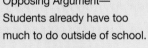

Transfer Your Learning

Across the Strands

Media Literacy: Many media texts also use generalization text pattern—for example, documentaries or news shows. What important questions should you ask when you watch or listen to a media text using this pattern?

Across the Curriculum

History: What support can you provide for this generalization: Explorers from France found many barriers to setting up a colony in Canada?

Talk About It

What do you already know about the Bermuda Triangle?

THE MYSTERIOUS BERMUDA TRIANGLE
Theory and Myth

Nonfiction Article by Hillary Mayell

Generalization Text Pattern ↗

Generalization text pattern can be used for essays, speeches, newspaper editorials, or nonfiction articles. What do you think will be the focus of this nonfiction article?

Generalization Text Pattern →

A generalization text pattern organizes information into a general statement followed by facts, reasons, or examples that are intended to support it. What generalization is made in this paragraph?

On a sunny day in 1945, five Navy planes took off from their base in Florida on a routine training mission, known as Flight 19. Neither the planes nor the crew were ever seen again.

Thus, a legend was born. The Bermuda Triangle is an area roughly bounded by Miami, Bermuda, and Puerto Rico. No one keeps statistics, but in the last century, many ships and planes have simply vanished without a trace within the imaginary triangle.

Many exotic theories have been used to explain what happened to the missing travellers. The disappearances have been attributed to enormous sea monsters, giant squid, or extraterrestrials.

The reality, say many, is far more ordinary. They argue that nature (tsunamis, for example), human error, and just plain bad luck can explain the many disappearances.

"The region is highly travelled and has been a busy crossroads since the early days of European exploration," said John Reilly, a historian with the U.S. Naval Historical Foundation. "To say quite a few ships and airplanes have gone down there is like saying there are an awful lot of car accidents on Highway 401—surprise, surprise."

Graveyard of the Atlantic

The Bermuda Triangle region has some unusual features. In this region, a magnetic compass points toward true north instead of magnetic north. The difference between the two changes by as much as 20 degrees as one travels around the Earth. If this variation is not compensated for, a navigator could veer far off course quite quickly.

This area is also home to some of the deepest underwater trenches in the world. Treacherous shoals and reefs can be found along the continental shelf. Strong currents over the reefs constantly breed new navigational hazards.

Then there's the weather as a theory for why so many ships have disappeared. The Gulf Stream is like a 70- to 80-km-wide river within the ocean. It can cause disruptive weather and stormy seas that capsize ships.

Generalization Text Pattern →

When a generalization is made, support is required to justify it. What support is provided here?

Generalization Text Pattern →

Generalization text pattern may use certain words such as *theory* or *argument*. What words in this article help you identify the pattern?

"If you have the right atmospheric conditions, you could get quite unexpectedly high waves," said Dave Feit, of the U.S. National Oceanic and Atmospheric Administration's Marine Prediction Center. "If wave heights are three metres outside of the Gulf Stream, they could be two or even three times higher within it."

Still, given a choice between the horrifying idea of a giant squid's tentacles wrestling an innocent ship to the sea floor, or an alien abduction, versus human error, shoddy engineering, and a temperamental nature—who could resist the legend of the Bermuda Triangle?

And Flight 19? Well, it looks like they just ran out of gas. It was a training flight, after all.

← **Generalization Text Pattern**

Sometimes authors will include opposing points, so the reader understands both sides of the argument. What are the opposing points in this selection? How does the writer feel about the opposing points?

Reflecting

Analyzing Text Pattern: What arguments supported this author's generalization?

Metacognition: Do you think you understand generalization text pattern well enough to be able to identify it? Could you write a piece using it?

Critical Literacy: Did this selection convince you that the Bermuda Triangle can be explained by natural causes? Explain.

Talk About It

What do you think of when you hear the word *quest*?

THE MYSTERY OF THE FRANKLIN EXPEDITION

Nonfiction Article by Owen Beattie and John Geiger
from *Buried in Ice: The Mystery of a Lost Arctic Expedition*

In 1845, ship voyages to South Asia, around South America or Africa, were long and dangerous (see green lines). The British wanted to find a shorter, quicker route through North America (see dotted red line below).

On this map, the red lines show Franklin's route in 1845.

Background Information on the Franklin Expedition

For centuries explorers had dreamed of finding the Northwest Passage: a ship route to the riches of Asia across the seas in Canada's far north. Again and again, ships would sail for the Arctic—only to be trapped for long, dark months in a world of ice mountains and eerie lights.

In the spring of 1845 it seemed as if nothing could stop Sir John Franklin's expedition from finding the Passage. Crowds cheered and waved as the two ships sailed from England. But none of Franklin's crew would ever return home alive.

Their disappearance led to the greatest rescue missions ever attempted. During these searches a number of grisly discoveries were made and, in 1850, the graves of three sailors were discovered on the shore of tiny Beechey Island.

But the biggest questions remained unanswered. Where were Sir John and the rest of his men? Where were Sir John's ships: the *Erebus* and the *Terror*? And how could the greatest Arctic expedition of all time have ended in such tragedy?

Death in the Arctic

Clues began to appear as the searches continued. One searcher was Dr. John Rae, a Canadian explorer. In 1854 he met a group of Inuit who had silver forks and spoons from the Franklin expedition, as well as one of Franklin's own medals. They told Rae they had heard tales from other Inuit about forty white men walking south, and then collapsing from starvation.

Dr. Rae hurried to England to report his sad news, but he was not able to answer all the questions asked of him. He had not actually visited the scenes described to him by the Inuit, and many people doubted the accuracy of his reports. In 1857, Sir John Franklin's wife, Lady Jane Franklin, hired Captain Francis Leopold M'Clintock to find out whether Rae's story was true.

Captain M'Clintock journeyed to King William Island to look for signs of the expedition. In 1859 he found more remains and in a rock "cairn" (a pile of stones heaped up as a tomb) he discovered two notes written on a single piece of paper.

In 1854, Dr. John Rae met with a group of Inuit who had heard of a group of white men trying to walk out of the Arctic.

This dramatic painting shows the crew of the *Terror* preparing the ship for its first winter at Beechey Island. By spring, most of the sailors were dead.

What the Notes Said

The first note was dated May 28, 1847. It reported that the expedition had spent its first winter at Beechey Island and its second winter off the coast of King William Island. But around the margin of the paper was a second message.

Written nearly a year later this message described how the *Erebus* and the *Terror* had been trapped in ice off King William Island from September 12, 1846 to April 26, 1848. During that time, 24 men had died, including Sir John Franklin.

The note added that the 105 survivors were planning to walk south in the hopes of reaching the Back River. They thought they could then row up the inland river system to the nearest fur trade fort. After nearly two years, the men were finally forced to desert their ships in a last desperate struggle for survival as their food supplies declined.

Doomed March

The journey south was one that none of the men would complete. On King William Island, M'Clintock found another group of Inuit who described seeing a wrecked ship and told of seeing Englishmen who "fell down and died as they walked."

On the island's southern coast, M'Clintock found the evidence everyone had been looking for. On a beach ridge, he came across a bleached white human skeleton dressed in the shreds of a steward's uniform. Close by lay a small clothes brush and pocket comb.

In 1848, Franklin's sailors made a desperate attempt to walk to safety. Starving and exhausted, they dragged their boats south until they could go no farther.

Final proof of their doomed march was found at a spot along the coast that was later to be known as the "Boat Place."

There, M'Clintock came upon a lifeboat from one of Franklin's ships. The heavy boat was mounted on a sled. Inside the boat, along with huge amounts of supplies that included everything from button polish and heavy cookstoves, were two human skeletons.

For Franklin's men, the rescue had come eleven years too late. M'Clintock returned to England with news of his discoveries and after that, public interest in the Franklin mystery died down. But not completely.

Even in July it can seem like winter in the Arctic. This summer snowstorm took us [Owen Beattie and his crew] by surprise and we had no place to go for shelter except back to our tents.

Owen Beattie's Theory

In 1984, the tragedy still haunted the imagination of anthropologist Owen Beattie. He thought he knew what had gone wrong, but he needed proof. In the following pages, Owen Beattie describes his quest to find the evidence that would prove his theories

Owen Beattie's Account

For years people blamed scurvy (a lack of Vitamin C) and starvation for the disastrous end of the Franklin expedition. Bones I had previously examined certainly indicated that scurvy was a factor but I wondered what else I might discover.

I submitted small samples of the bones for element testing, a scientific process that measures the presence of different elements contained in human bone.

I was astonished by what the tests revealed—high levels of lead. In fact, there was so much lead in the bone that it was probable that this sailor had been poisoned by it.

Lead is a metal that is very dangerous when eaten or inhaled. In large enough doses it can even kill a person. Smaller amounts damage certain organs in the body and can interfere with how people think and behave. A person can actually go mad from the effects of lead.

Had this sailor taken in the lead during the voyage or before? Had other members of the expedition also suffered from deadly amounts of this metal?

To answer these questions I needed more than just skeletal remains. What I needed to examine was soft tissue—skin, muscle, hair, and organs from members of Franklin's doomed crew.

I knew there was only one place where I had a chance of finding such tissues preserved in the frozen Arctic ground. And so I had come to inspect the three graves that had been dug almost 140 years ago on the shores of Beechey Island.

View of graves from the plane.

Frozen Forensics

"I can see the graves!" I shouted to the pilot as we approached Beechey Island. The tiny dark points on the gravel-covered island could only be one thing—the grave markers of three young sailors who had died on Sir John Franklin's expedition: John Hartnell, William Braine, and John Torrington.

These men were the astronauts of their time, risking everything in the name of science and adventure. Had they conquered the Northwest Passage, they would have been hailed as heroes. Instead, they lay buried on an icy shore thousands of kilometres from home.

Would the sailor's bodies be well enough preserved to provide the final clue to what had gone so wrong?

It was like a scene from a horror movie, I thought to myself. In the gnawing Arctic cold, as the wind ripped around us and a massive black cloud rolled in over the site, our team hacked through 1.5 m of cement-hard frozen earth.

The air around the site was quiet, even solemn, as we finally exposed a coffin. There, perfectly preserved in the permafrost was the sailor, John Torrington. Suddenly, I felt tremendous sadness for this young man's passing. Each one of us, I think, was imagining what this man's final days must have been like.

During the next four hours, we examined the body and collected bone, hair, and tissue samples for later analysis. After we were finished, we carefully laid Torrington's body back in the coffin. The lid was replaced. Water, seeping naturally back into the grave, would soon freeze and seal it again.

Photos and grids helped us to reconstruct the sailor's graves. It was important to leave them exactly as we'd found them.

In the 19th century, many Britons believed that their way of dressing and eating was superior. This belief contributed to how unprepared Franklin's crew were. In this painting, you can see that the sailors are not dressed for harsh, cold weather.

The Mystery Solved

In early 1987 the test results were ready at last. Lab tests on bone and tissue samples from all three sailors showed excessively high lead content. An analysis of the hair samples proved that these men had suffered from acute lead poisoning while they were on the Franklin expedition.

During most of the nineteenth century, tins were sealed shut with a mixture of lead and tin called *solder*. I knew that Sir John Franklin's expedition had been loaded full of food packed in tin cans—8000 of them. But the cans Franklin carried were seriously flawed.

The metal edges and seams of the cans were sealed *on the inside* with large pieces of solder made of melted lead and tin. While the can was full, lethal doses of lead from the solder would have dissolved into the food.

I was struck by the horrifying truth—lead had contributed to the declining health of the entire crews of the *Erebus* and the *Terror*.

Not only did the sailors suffer from loss of appetite, weakness, and other physical symptoms of lead poisoning, but the lead probably also affected their minds, making them behave strangely. Many of them may have been unusually irritable, filled with unreal fears, incapable of clear thoughts, and unable to make important decisions.

Our research also proved that the composition of the lead in the bodies and in the canned foods was identical. How ironic it was, I thought, that the canned foods which should have allowed the men to survive were instead the cause of the early deaths of many sailors.

rusted food can from Beechey Island

This painting shows a burial service being held for one of the sailors who died early in the expedition. To reach the grave the sailors had to strap the coffin to a sled and haul it over hills of ice.

The men aboard Franklin's expedition expected to succeed, in part because they carried the latest technology of Queen Victoria's time. And yet they died as a result of one of those new inventions.

Lead poisoning was certainly not the only cause of the Franklin disaster. Once the supply of food ran out, starvation and scurvy claimed the last survivors. But it was the lead hidden in the food supply that slowly poisoned them all, playing an important role in the poor health and judgment that doomed the famous expedition.

When Sir John Franklin sailed from the River Thames in May 1845, an entire nation believed the honour of charting the Northwest Passage was within his grasp. None could have guessed that inside the tins stored within the ship's hold there lurked a time bomb just as dangerous for the crew as the cruel Arctic winter.

Reflecting

Analyzing Text Pattern: Owen Beattie's generalization is that Franklin and his crew didn't die from scurvy, but from lead poisoning. How is that generalization supported? What background information helps you understand the generalization?

Metacognition: How does your understanding of physical geography and climate give you a better understanding of the events described in this selection?

Connecting to Other Media: What images from the selection or elsewhere would you use to create a photo essay about the Franklin Expedition?

Science and Technology

The reading strategy you learned in this unit can help you better understand text in other subject areas. As you read this science article, make connections and look for clues to help you make inferences.

Acid Snails

Online Science Article by Emily Sohn

Human activities have a major impact on the rest of the creatures sharing this planet, including those in our oceans: from the snail to the whale. Because all creatures are interconnected, something that seems insignificant can have major consequences.

Conditions in the world's oceans are changing, as a result of human activities. Those changes might be affecting the ability of a small snail to defend itself, suggests a new study.

Factories, cars, and other machines spit out lots of a gas called *carbon dioxide*. Carbon dioxide (CO_2) is known as a greenhouse gas because it traps heat in the atmosphere. More and more of the gas has been accumulating in the air in recent years.

Carbon dioxide has also been dissolving in seawater, and that's been changing the water's chemical composition. As a result, seawater at the surface of the world's oceans has become more acidic. That shift could eventually make life tougher for a type of snail called the *common periwinkle*, say researchers from the University of Plymouth in England.

Common periwinkles are able to grow thicker shells when predators are near, unless the seawater becomes too acidic.

The common periwinkle lives along coastlines throughout much of Europe. One of its main predators is the common shore crab. The hungry crabs grab the snails "like ice cream cones," says lead researcher Simon Rundle. Snails with thin shells are most likely to get crushed and eaten.

Scientists already knew that snails grow thicker shells to protect themselves when predators live nearby. The British researchers wanted to know if an increase in the acidity of the water would affect this thickening process.

The scientists grew more than 100 periwinkles in four tanks. They put half the snails in tanks filled with normal seawater. The other half were placed in tanks that had carbon dioxide added to the water to make it acidic. The researchers then placed a crab in each of two tanks: one containing the normal seawater, the other containing the acidic seawater.

In the tanks with normal seawater, the periwinkle shells grew substantially thicker when a crab was living at the bottom. In the tanks with acidic water, the snail shells did not get thicker. These results suggest that snails living in acidic water have a harder time defending themselves from predators.

25 periwinkles in normal seawater, no crab

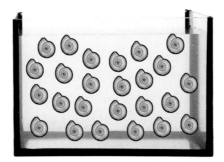

25 periwinkles in acidic seawater, no crab

25 periwinkles in normal seawater, with crab

25 periwinkles in acidic seawater, with crab

Scientists measure acidity on what's called the pH scale. A liquid with a pH of 7, such as distilled water, is considered neutral. A pH measurement of less than 7 indicates acidity. Lemon juice and stomach acid are examples of acidic substances. A pH of greater than 7 is the opposite of acidic, often called basic or alkaline. Bleach is one example.

Overall, the oceans are slightly alkaline, with a pH of about 8. Studies show that the pH of ocean water has dropped in the past few hundred years. Computer models suggest that ocean pH could drop even more.

That change could be a problem for all sorts of underwater organisms. As seawater becomes more acidic, these creatures have an increasingly difficult time producing a mineral called *calcium carbonate*. This material makes up coral reefs, sea urchin teeth, and snail shells, among other structures

Until now, studies of seawater acidity have mostly looked at its effects on individual species. The new study shows that changes in the oceans are influencing interactions between species, too.

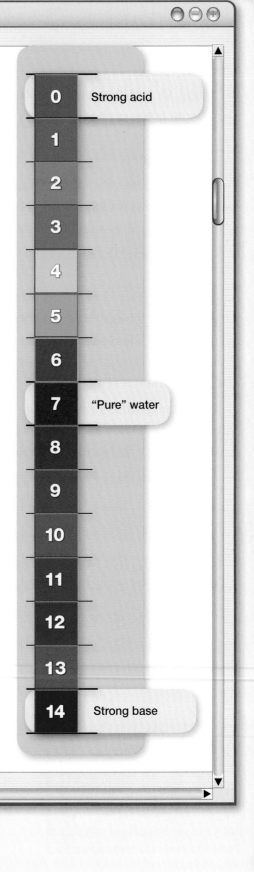

0 — Strong acid
1
2
3
4
5
6
7 — "Pure" water
8
9
10
11
12
13
14 — Strong base

Reflecting

Making Inferences: What inferences did you make as you read this science article? What clues in the text helped you make inferences?

Metacognition: How did the diagram and scale help you understand the article? What other information would you find useful? What background information helped you make inferences?

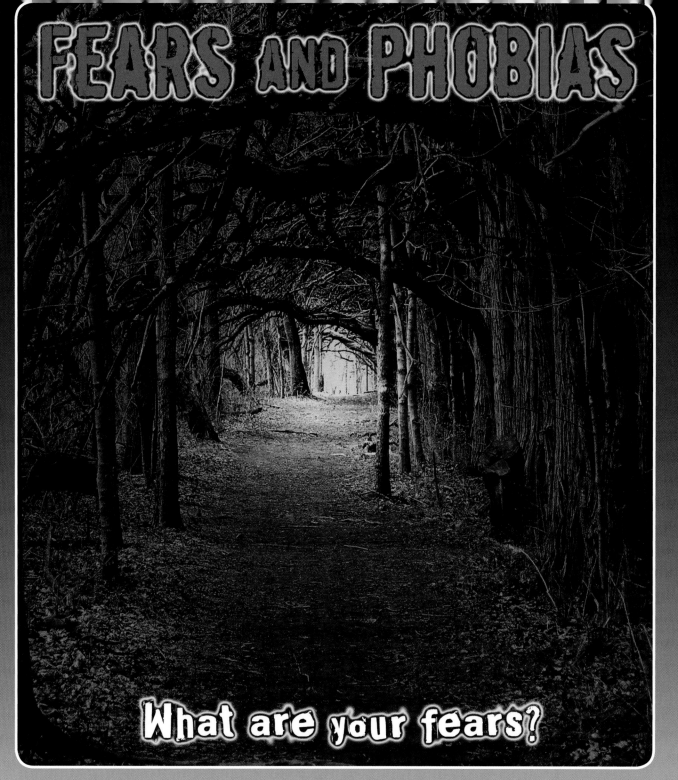

FEARS AND PHOBIAS

What are your fears?

Unit Learning Goals

- summarize important ideas while reading
- improve word choice while writing

- summarize while listening
- identify point of view in media texts

- analyze nonfiction recount text pattern

Transfer Your Learning: Health

How to > Summarize

Here is an example of a graphic organizer to summarize a selection that uses a descriptive text pattern.

Detail

Detail

Detail

Main Topic

Detail

Detail

When you create a summary for a selection, you reduce the text to its main ideas. Summarizing is a good strategy to help you understand the author's message and the ideas that support the message. Summarizing can help you study, since it helps you focus on and remember important information.

1. After you've read the whole text, identify the author's message— the main idea of the whole text. Text features, like the title, topic sentence, or photos, can help you.

2. In each paragraph or section, identify the key idea for that section and the details that support it. The key idea for a section is related to the main idea of the whole text. Often the key idea is in the first or last sentence of a section. Headings or subheadings can also reveal the key idea.

3. Identify only those details that are important to the key idea. Ignore details that are not important.

4. Sometimes long lists of items can be replaced with one word or a shorter phrase.

5. Create a summary of the text in your own words. Make sure you include a topic sentence and a closing statement or remark.

Transfer Your Learning

Across the Strands

Writing: How does what you've just learned connect to what you learned about narrowing the topic in Unit 1?

Across the Curriculum

Health: Magazines and newspapers often include long articles that tell you what you need to do to stay healthy. Why would you want to summarize the information in these articles?

Talk About It

What are the advantages of feeling afraid?

PHOBIA FACTOR

**Nonfiction Article by
Lachlan Kirkwood**

Summarizing ⬆

Identify the author's message. What does this title tell you about the main idea of this selection?

Summarizing ➡

Identify the key idea and supporting details in this paragraph. In one sentence, how would you summarize this paragraph?

Fears and Phobias

Believe it or not, *fear* can help us succeed in the world. It all starts when we are babies. That is when we learn to fear—and avoid—situations that aren't safe. For example, we might cry if we're in a high place where we could fall. As we get older we continue to learn to fear dangerous situations and to avoid those situations that cause us danger. Fear is a natural reaction to danger. It protects us. Without fear, imagine the trouble we'd be in!

heat: thermophobia

spiders: arachnophobia

needles: belonophobia

shadows: sciophobia

Summarizing

Identify details that are important and ignore details that are not important. Decide what details in this paragraph are important.

school: scholionophobia

thinking: phronephobia

being dirty: autophobia

machinery: mechanophobia

colour: chromatophobia or chromophobia

Fortunately, for most of us, fear is just a small part of our lives. That is because our fears are based on *reasonable* dangers. If we are in a dangerous situation and feel afraid, our fear usually goes away when the danger ends.

Unfortunately, for some people, fears are extreme. About 5% of the population has a *phobia*—an extreme feeling of fear. A phobia is an *excessive* or unreasonable fear of an object, place, or situation. Unlike fears that help us *avoid* dangers (like high places or dangerous animals) these fears aren't usually based on real threats. Phobias are so strong that, instead of helping us the way most fears do, they hurt us by disrupting our daily lives.

Many Types of Phobias

There are many different kinds of phobias. The most common is called *social phobia*. People with social phobia have an intense fear of interacting with, or being in front of, other people. If faced with a situation that sparks this phobia, these people can become so stressed that they feel physically sick. Kids with social phobia are terrified of talking to a teacher or speaking in front of the class. Even walking across the room to the pencil sharpener might bring out their phobia.

Agoraphobia (pronounced uh-GORE-uh-FO-bee-uh) is another common phobia. People who suffer from agoraphobia have a fear of being in open or public places, especially if those places are crowded. This fear can be so intense that sometimes they refuse to leave their own homes. Imagine how hard life would be if we couldn't leave home!

Many people have specific phobias of certain objects or situations. Common examples include ophidiophobia (oh-FI-dee-oh-fo-bee-uh—fear of snakes), apiphobia (APE-uh-fo-bee-uh—fear of bees), acrophobia (AH-kro-fo-bee-uh—fear of heights), or aviophobia (AY-vee-oh-fo-bee-uh—fear of flying). You probably already know a lot of other specific phobias, but check out the list in the thorns on these pages! Most of these phobias develop when we're kids, but may go away in time. However, if these phobias last or get worse, expert help may be needed!

Symptoms of Phobias

People who suffer from phobias may have some of these symptoms:

- unrealistic worry about a situation or object that seems harmless to most people

- anxiety accompanied by a strong physical reaction, such as a racing heart, sweating, trembling, or nausea

- an overwhelming urge to flee the situation

← Summarizing

Replace long lists with a single word or short phrase. What word or phrase can summarize this list of items?

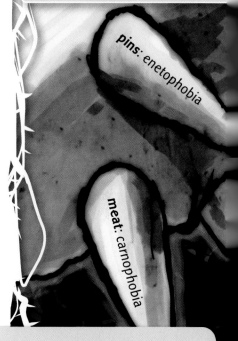

pins: enetophobia

meat: carnophobia

strangers: xenophobia

mirrors: eisoptrophobia

Check out these famous people and their phobias.

Thomas Edison invented the lightbulb and was afraid of the dark (nyctophobia).

Madonna, famous and seemingly fearless singer, has a fear of thunder (brontophobia).

Aretha Franklin, singer, is afraid of flying (aviophobia).

David Beckham, soccer star, is afraid of disorder (ataxophobia).

Natalie Wood, an actor from the 1960s, was deathly afraid of water (aquaphobia). She died by drowning.

Rupert Grint, actor (*Harry Potter*), has a fear of spiders (arachnophobia).

Oprah Winfrey, talk-show host, is afraid of chewing gum (chiclephobia).

Anne Rice, horror writer, is afraid of the dark (nyctophobia).

Ray Bradbury, famous science fiction author, is afraid of flying (aviophobia).

Summarizing

→

In each section, identify the key idea and supporting details. How does the heading help you identify the important details in this section?

odours: osmophobia or olfactophobia

Summarizing

Create a summary of the text using your own words. How can the headings in this selection help you organize a summary?

Summarizing

→

This selection uses descriptive text pattern. At right is a good graphic organizer for organizing summary notes for this text.

Treatment

One way to treat a person with phobias is with *exposure therapy*. With this method, patients are slowly exposed to their fears. They become increasingly comfortable with whatever they fear through gradual exposures. So, for example, someone who fears snakes might begin by reading about snakes. Once they're used to reading about snakes, they would move on to looking at photos of snakes, then looking at snakes in an aquarium, then touching a snake with gloves, and finally holding one with bare hands. With this treatment, patients work through increasingly difficult situations and learn that nothing bad happens. They learn to manage, and eventually overcome, their fear.

Virtual reality technology is a great tool during exposure therapy. Exposure to some fears, such as the fear of flying, could be expensive and time consuming. So therapists use virtual reality to give patients repeated exposure to flying without having them board an airplane!

The length of treatment depends on the person, but generally most people respond very well to treatment and go on to live normal, happy, and productive lives—fear-free at last!

symptoms

types

phobias

treatment

Reflecting

Summarizing: What summarizing strategies did you use as you read this article? How did summarizing help you understand this article?

Metacognition: How does understanding your own fears affect your ability to understand the information in this article?

Talk About It
Some people are afraid of snakes, flying, or spiders.
Other people are afraid they've left the iron turned on.

My Maturity, in FLAMES

Personal Anecdote by M.T. Anderson

Not far from where I live now, there is a town where ancient houses stand around a quiet green, a town with views that sweep all the way from Massachusetts to the mountains of Vermont and New Hampshire. A friend of mine lived there, and once, when she and her parents were going to be away for several weeks, they asked me whether I could live in their house for them while they were gone and make sure it weathered the snow.

I was perhaps seventeen. I had never lived alone. This was exciting. They were gone, and the house was mine. I walked in the front door and spread my arms out. The windows looked out over a landscape of pines and ice. I felt that I was master of all I surveyed.

I have always been somewhat of an incompetent, so I was determined to get this right. For two weeks, I treated that house gingerly and lovingly. I watered the geraniums. I washed all the dishes by hand. I avoided making any impression on the cushions. I didn't move anything, not even the baleful, curly-haired china doll that they left, for some ungodly reason, glaring down the steps at me from the attic, just waiting for me to go to sleep so it could sink its little porcelain fangs into my hamstrings.

Occasionally, I would drop cheerful little notes to my friend's parents, saying things like, "Don't worry about a thing. Everything's fine here. Incidentally, would you call the brick wall in the living room a 'structural' wall? Just wondering. Hope to hear from you soon! –MTA."

At the end of the two weeks, I was startled to discover that I had behaved responsibly the whole time. I hadn't blown it. Nothing was broken.

I cleaned the place up and prepared to leave. Knowing that I have a tendency to worry—I had, once, when twelve, alerted a whole London neighbourhood to the presence of an asthmatic serial killer who turned out to be a loose awning—I double-checked everything that could possibly go wrong in the house. The basement was dry. All of the burners on the stove were off. The back door was locked. I loaded my car and prepared to drive away.

Suddenly, it occurred to me that I hadn't checked the iron. I got out of the car, unlocked the front door, ran upstairs, and checked the iron. It was off. I ran downstairs, shut the front door, got in the car, looked at the front door, got out of the car, went to the front door, rattled the front door to make sure it was locked, got back into the car, and drove away.

I had only gone a mile or two when I began to feel like something was wrong. The iron. Sometimes it is not clear if you have checked a heating element *enough*.

I should perhaps mention at this point that I had never used the iron while at the house. I had never touched it before I checked it. This made it unlikely that the iron was on.

But some irons are actually activated by movement. When you pick them up, they turn on. Maybe checking the iron had been the very thing that caused it to heat up.

This was patently ridiculous. Thinking back, I dimly remembered actually unplugging the iron when I checked it. At least, upon reflection, I thought I remembered unplugging it. I drove on.

Resolutely, I decided that, as I had never used the iron, if it was on, it was not my fault. The iron would have to have been on since the family left two weeks ago. If the house burned down, it was technically their fault.

But they wouldn't know that. They would think I had left the iron on. They would hate me. They would walk through the blackened ruins of their beautiful home and hiss my name.

But I had checked the iron. I was almost entirely sure that it hadn't been on. Unless it came on from jiggling. In the way that some do. I thought.

I was now a half an hour away from the house. I could still call the next-door neighbours and ask them to check. But that would blow my cool. "Could you break into the house next door and see if I left the iron on … which I never used?"

No, I thought. *I will be an adult. I will not cave in to this fantasy.*

I turned on the radio to something soothing. The slow movement of a Mozart piano concerto. *This*, I thought, *is what adults listen to, instead of the raving paranoiac voices within them.*

It was a big mistake. Because it turns out that the slow movement of a Mozart piano concerto—with all its lilt and elegance—is, to someone in my state, precisely the soundtrack for disaster. It is just the kind of pleasant, polite music you hear in a movie when someone is smiling to himself, driving away from a house where he has stayed for two weeks, and then you cut to the iron setting fire to the ironing board cover. Then you flash back to the kid in the car, contented, tapping time to the Mozart, and then back to the flaming curtains, then back to the kid going down the highway, waving at some toddlers in the back of a minivan, then back to the house completely in flames, the fire department kicking in the door, screaming, timbers falling; and, just as the slow movement of the Mozart piano concerto ends, a shot of the glowing embers, with the china doll smiling up out of the ruins.

I stopped at a gas station. I called the neighbours. They weren't home. I begged their answering machine to go check the iron. I blathered to the answering machine that I hadn't used the iron, but maybe instead of turning it off when I checked it, I had turned it on—I asked the neighbours this and many more favours—and I hoped that during adulthood, things would be different, that things would be sure and safe—the irons upright, the Mozart calm, the doll, at long last, entombed inside a trunk— that things, by then, would not always be on fire.

Oh well.

Reflecting

Summarizing: Summarize this selection in a couple of sentences.

Metacognition: M.T. Anderson thinks about his own thinking in this anecdote. What metacognitive strategies does he use? How effective are they?

Critical Literacy: How would this story be different if told by the neighbours or the owners of the house?

68   Unit 4: Fears and Phobias

NEL

Talk About It

"Fear is the emotion that makes us blind."

KiNg oN FeaR

Essay by Stephen King

Let's talk, you and I. Let's talk about fear.

The house is empty as I write this; a cold February rain is falling outside. It's night. Sometimes when the wind blows the way it's blowing now, we lose the power. But for now it's on, and so let's talk very honestly about fear. Let's talk very rationally about moving to the rim of madness … and perhaps over the edge.

My name is Stephen King. I am a grown man with a wife and three children. I love them, and I believe that the feeling is reciprocated. My job is writing, and it's a job I like very much. My novels have been successful enough to allow me to write full-time, which is an agreeable thing to be able to do.

Still … let's talk about fear. We won't raise our voices and we won't scream; we'll talk rationally, you and I. We'll talk about the way the good fabric of things sometimes has a way of unravelling with shocking suddenness.

At night, when I go to bed, I still am at pains to be sure that my legs are under the blankets after the lights go out. I'm not a child anymore, but ... I don't like to sleep with one leg sticking out. Because if a cool hand ever reached out from under the bed and grasped my ankle, I might scream. Yes, I might scream to wake the dead. That sort of thing doesn't happen, of course, and we all know that. In my stories you will encounter all manner of night creatures: vampires, demon lovers, a thing that lives in the closet, all sorts of other terrors. None of them are real. The thing under my bed waiting to grab my ankle isn't real. I know that, and I also know that if I'm careful to keep my foot under the covers, it will never be able to grab my ankle.

There is an old fable about seven blind men who grabbed seven different parts of an elephant. One of them thought he had a snake, one of them thought he had a giant palm leaf, one of them thought he was touching a stone pillar. When they got together, they decided they had an elephant.

Fear is the emotion that makes us blind. How many things are we afraid of? We're afraid to turn off the lights when our hands are wet. We're afraid to stick a knife into the toaster to get the stuck English muffin without unplugging it first. We're afraid of what the doctor may tell us when the physical exam is over; when the airplane suddenly takes a great unearthly lurch in midair. We're afraid that the oil may run out, that the good air will run out, the good water, the good life. When the daughter promised to be in by eleven and it's now quarter past twelve and sleet is spatting against the window like dry sand, we sit and pretend to watch television and look occasionally at the mute telephone and we feel the emotion that makes us blind, the emotion that makes a stealthy ruin of the thinking process.

UNABRIDGED

STEPHEN KING

READ BY
RON McLARTY

STATIONARY BIKE

The infant is a fearless creature only until the first time the mother isn't there when he cries. The toddler quickly discovers the blunt and painful truths of the slamming door, the hot burner, the fever that goes with the croup or the measles. Children learn fear quickly; they pick it up off the mother or father's face when the parent comes into the bathroom and sees them with the bottle of pills or the safety razor.

Fear makes us blind, and we touch each fear with all the avid curiosity of self-interest, trying to make a whole out of a hundred parts, like the blind men with their elephant.

When you read horror, you don't really believe what you read. You don't believe in vampires, werewolves, trucks that suddenly start up and drive themselves. We are, in our real everyday worlds, often like the masks of Comedy and Tragedy, grinning on the outside, grimacing on the inside. There's a central switching point somewhere inside, a transformer, maybe, where the wires leading from those two masks connect. And that is the place where the horror story so often hits home.

The tale of monstrosity and terror is a basket loosely packed with phobias; when the writer passes by, you take one of his imaginary horrors out of the basket and put one of your real ones in—at least for a time.

Reflecting

Summarizing: In no more than four sentences, how would you summarize this essay? What key points would you choose for your summary? Why?

Metacognition: How did summarizing this essay affect your understanding of it? Did summarizing help you remember the essay?

Critical Literacy: Why do you think Stephen King wrote this essay about fear? How would different audiences respond to this essay? For example, a reader who loves Stephen's books and a reader who hates his books.

Talk About It
What's the difference between fear and terror?

Fear!....

Short Story by Budge Wilson

This is what the shrink said. Well, he's not exactly a shrink. He's a counsellor. He counsels. He advises. He suggests. He asks questions—questions we don't have to answer. He takes us down paths that lead somewhere. His name is Adrien O'Malley. We don't call him Adrien. We call him Mr. O'Malley. "A little distance can be good," he said last week at the end of our first meeting, and then added, "Call me Mr. O'Malley." This isn't what I meant by "what the shrink said." I'll get to that in a minute. I need to tell you some other stuff first.

I'm in this school group that meets every Thursday afternoon. It's the only day when there isn't something like hockey or soccer or art or music, which, of course, I'd be too scared to try out for anyway. It's a free afternoon for all the Grade 8s except us. One day when I was standing outside the staff room, waiting for Mrs. Hugo to hand me out a note, I could hear the teachers talking about our group. I knew it was us they were talking about, because they named names. They called us the VCDs or sometimes VCs. The real VC stands for Victoria Cross, which is a very high level award for bravery (I think maybe you have to die to get it, but I'm not sure. If so, I wouldn't call that much of an inducement if you wanted to collect a chestful of medals). After lurking around outside the staff room and keeping my ears wide open for several days, I was able to discover that VCD stands for Visible and Chronic Defects.

So I'm in this group of kids with visible and chronic defects. Of course we're visible. Otherwise, how would they know to put us in the group? And of course we're chronic (which basically means on and on and on, forever) or else they could just wait until we stopped being what we are. Our defects are pretty straightforward and easy to define—but apparently not easy to correct. Most of the defects are anger, fear, anxiety, and violence. I've been in this school long enough to know that some of the school's scariest bullies have all four of these defects. So you can see right off why it's often so hard to cure a bully of being a bully.

Our group is made up of five boys. This isn't because girls don't have any defects. They have their own VCD group. That's because the school principal thinks we'll feel freer to talk about our problems among our own gender. He doesn't like to use the word *sex*, which makes me wonder if he has a chunk of chronic anxiety himself.

My own defect is fear. I've got fear in a big way. I'm so fearful of so many things that even anxiety looks easy. Anxiety is being worried. Being worried all the time is probably not great, but to me it looks easy. Put anxiety and fear on the table together, and figure out the difference between them. Anxiety is walking around on little sharp pebbles in a pair of shoes with very thin soles. Fear is walking on a pile of nails in your bare feet. Terror is when the sharp parts of the nails are sticking straight up. Sometimes I feel terror. Then I don't walk anywhere, in case there might be some nails around.

Apart from walking on nails, I'll give you a short version of what fear is like. It's having a heart that does a lot of hyperactive pounding. It's having a mouth go so dry when someone speaks to you (like a teacher or an uncle or a total stranger asking for directions to the Halifax Shopping Centre) that you don't get a single word out. Or you stutter and tremble, which is worse. It's not ever daring to go to a party, or try out for a play, or say hello to Annika Setko. It's feeling jittery the minute you wake up in the morning, before anything even happens.

The only thing I can do without fear is write. That's because there's just me and the page. I've written in so many journals that I have to keep my clothes on the floor of my closet because all my drawers are full of my diaries.

So far, in this VCD group, we haven't had to talk. That probably comes later. Maybe soon— I will try not to think about it.

So now I get to what Mr. O'Malley said. On the second Thursday—yesterday—after we got to know him a bit, he said, "I'm going to give you your main assignment. It's open-ended. The only requirement is that you have to fill one exercise book by the time the March break rolls around. In it, you'll be talking about your most visible problem for thirty-two pages. That will be your only subject matter. You could cheat by writing big. Or you could fill your notebook with useless stuff. Like what you eat for breakfast or whether you like blonds better than redheads. Don't do that. This isn't a diary. This is therapy. If you don't know what that means, look it up in the dictionary."

Then he just stood there and looked at us for a few moments, as though he was waiting for all that to sink in. Next, he went over and stood beside a flip chart he keeps at the front of the room. The first thing he wrote on it was WHO I AM, in very big letters.

"But before you start your major assignment, write that down," he said, "and then get ready to describe yourself. Not just your problem. Anything. Everything. How old you are. What your family's like. If your family has just one parent or none, say so. If you're with a foster family, say so. If you hate spinach and love ice cream, say so. Here's your chance to tell me what you eat for breakfast and if you prefer blonds. Describe how tall you are, how handsome, how ugly, whether you wear glasses, who decides what clothes you wear, who likes you, who doesn't, what you do in your spare time. I'm not requiring you to talk yet, so I need some other way to get to know you."

Mr. O'Malley was silent for a moment. "Okay," he went on, "WHO I AM has to be done at home. I'd actually like to see it as soon as possible, so have it ready by next Thursday. I want at least three pages, single spaced."

Henry McLaughlin's eyes were wild. "Hey!" he actually shouted. "You said 'the March break!'" He looked ready to smash the desk with his fist, which was raised about fifteen centimetres above it. His knuckles were shiny and white. His hand—the one holding his pencil—was trembling.

"I'm sorry, Henry," said Mr. O'Malley, and he looked as if he really meant it. "I guess I misled you. Absolutely my fault. The part that I'm about to discuss with you will be due by the start of March break—the real heavy-duty assignment. But I'd like to have everyone's WHO I AM in my hands by next Thursday. I apologize for not making that clear."

Henry was so stunned to hear an apology coming out of someone who was almost a teacher that his hand stopped shaking and his mouth flew open. Mr. O'Malley continued on without a pause, facing us, making eye contact.

"Okay," he said. "Now comes the hard part. Or maybe not. Time will tell." He went to the flip chart again and wrote down PROBLEM.

"What we need to do now," he said, "is to think about the sorts of things you'll be talking about in your big assignment." He walked back to his chair and sat down opposite our semicircle of five desks. He looked at all of us.

"You know by now," he said, "what your main problem is, so write it down. If you punched four people last week, your most visible problem is violence. Write that down. In the course of these sessions and of this assignment, you may discover some other problems that cause that behaviour. We'll deal with that later. For now, stick with the most obvious."

I could see Henry McLaughlin writing down ANGER. I wrote down FEAR. The principal was right about the gender thing. It would have been impossible for me to write that down so openly, so nakedly, if that blond and curly-haired Annika Setko had been sitting in one of those five chairs. Not, mind you, that Annika Setko could ever be a VCD.

I watched the other guys out of the corner of my eye. Of course, being me, I was scared to look at them head-on. There was a lot of pencil rubbing and nail biting. They seemed to be having trouble identifying their problems. I saw George Thornbloom write down a big V—and then cross it out. He chewed his lip for a bit, and then wrote down ANGER. Two Angers and one Fear, I thought. Then Jamieson Freebury, who has almost no fingernails, wrote ANXIETY on his first page. Right afterwards, Donald Wilmington heaved a long, deep sigh and wrote the same thing. Having seen Donald in action, I expected to see him write ANGER or VIOLENCE (and certainly I was scared to death of him), but probably he decided that ANXIETY was safer. Which maybe, come to think of it, just shows how anxious he really is?

"Then," Mr. O'Malley said, "write down some of the things or people or experiences that make you angry or fearful or anxious or violent—that you think cause your problem. Make a list of those bits of information on the left-hand side of the page under the title CAUSES, leaving a few spaces under each item.

"At the top of the right-hand side of the page write WHY. Then write a reason opposite everything on your list. Let's just take one problem and do a sample."

He wrote on the flip chart.

PROBLEM
Anger

CAUSES	WHY
Brother	Too bossy
Homework	Too hard
	Too much
Team sports	Kids say I'm no good
	Everyone plays rough
Frustration	I want everything to be easy
	I want to win
Mother	Scolds me all the time
	Hates my haircut
Other kids	Too stupid
	I don't like them
	They're sissies
Sister	Spends too long in the bathroom
	Makes fun of me

I could hardly wait to start. I wanted like anything to write this stuff down. I knew what the things were that scared me. And some of the time I thought I knew why. But not often. I was even scared to be in this group. Why? I didn't know. I was scared to answer questions in class, even when I knew the answers. Why? I didn't know. But I knew I'd probably be filling six of those exercise notebooks before March.

But suddenly I was looking at an enormous fear, a terrifying thought. It was making me walk on all those upturned nails. Here it was: I needed to know if we'd have to let the other kids read our assignments, and I was scared to ask. But I KNEW I'D BE TOO FRIGHTENED TO WRITE DOWN ONE SINGLE WORD UNLESS I KNEW THE ANSWER TO THAT QUESTION. Why? Because I was afraid of what those kids would do with that information.

That added up to two fears. Which was worse? To ask the question or not to know the answer? Both were scary. But if I got rid of one, the other might go away. I did a lot of fast and very serious thinking.

My pencil was rat-tat-tatting against my desk. My heart skipped a bunch of beats. I hoped I wasn't having a heart attack.

I shut my eyes and put up my hand. It was one of the hardest things I ever did. I mean it.

"Yes, Peter," said Mr. O'Malley's friendly voice.

I could just barely get it out. But even though I stuttered a lot and had to cough quite a few times, I did it. What I said was, "Will the other kids see the stuff we write?"

"No," said Mr. O'Malley. "They won't."

I had killed one fear with another fear.

It was like a miracle. The weight that lifted off my head, my shoulders, my chest was as heavy as a truckful of lumber. Without it, I felt, for a minute, lighter than air. I was also aware of something tickling my funnybone. Here is what I was thinking: I'm in this room with two Anxieties and two Angers and a Shrink. What's more, one of the Anxieties is really a Violent. And right this second, none of them scares me. The real Anxiety may turn out to be a friend. His fingernails look exactly like mine. If I had a friend I'd feel safer. And I feel safe with Mr. O'Malley. Or almost safe. And maybe safe people are friends, even if they're the wrong age.

Mr. O'Malley was going on and on about the assignment, but I was only listening with a small slice of my brain. However, I got the drift. Obviously we were going to be thinking about and deciphering our separate problems from now until March. This was a little bit frightening, but not very. After all, I felt like I'd been thinking about my fears ever since the minute I was born. I feel bad about that. As a matter of fact, I feel bad most of the time. But no one ever asked that big WHY before. And now Mr. O'Malley was saying something really interesting. He said that in our assignment we should also write down some of the things that could make our problem less awful.

Already I was listing them in my head:

- Cats, because they move slowly and gracefully and purr when you stroke them. Also, they seem to like me. They come up to me on the street and rub my leg. I wish I had a cat. They make me almost calm.

- Storms, with waves crashing and trees blowing around. They make me feel better about my own rage. Rage? So I must be an Anger, too. Some of the time, anyway. Yes. Yes, I am.

- Old Mr. Corkum on Preston Street. He talks to me about being in the Second World War, and tells me about how you can feel brave and terrified all at the same time. I understand that now, because of the brave thing I just did—even though most people would think that the brave thing I did today was smaller than nothing.

I found myself writing my WHO I AM homework before Mr. O'Malley had even stopped talking. "I'm Peter Jefferson," I wrote. "I'm 14 years old, and I live in Halifax. I'm scared of just about everything—kids, grown-ups, most teachers, my father, my mother, my older brother, our huge dog, school, crowds, being alone, the dark, graveyards, traffic, sickness, dying. I'm scared most of the time. But for half an hour this afternoon I didn't feel any fear at all. That must mean something. I'm not sure what. But I'll tell you one thing—whatever it is, it's not something that I'm afraid of."

I was still writing after the other kids had left the class. I looked up at Mr. O'Malley, and we smiled at each other. Then I gathered up my books and backpack and left the room.

Reflecting

Summarizing: If you were telling a friend about this story, how would you summarize it?

Metacognition: The main character is asked to write about his problem. From your own experiences, explain how writing about a problem can change the way you think about that problem.

Critical Literacy: How do you think the author wants you to feel about the main character? What does the author do to get you to feel this way?

How to ➤ Improve Word Choice

When you revise your writing, you have the chance to improve your word choice. You make changes so that the ideas in your writing are conveyed to the reader as effectively as possible. Revision doesn't mean that there is anything wrong with your writing; just that you are working to make it even better than it was before.

1. Use very precise words for the message you want to send. Are you afraid of bugs … or are you afraid of large, hairy spiders?

2. Choose the right synonym for the mood or tone of the piece. The words *frightened*, *alarmed*, *terrified*, and *petrified* are similar in meaning, but each word gives the reader a different idea about how someone is feeling.

3. Show, don't tell. Choose words that can show your reader what you mean. Rather than just saying your character was scared, say … his legs were shaking, and every hair on his body had just jumped to attention.

4. Cross out unnecessary words that don't contribute to your message or mood.

Arachnophobia

~~Fear of Spiders~~ ⌄ ∧
Poem by Karri

The spider's ∧legs
        dangly

~~crawl~~ across the ∧page.
creep   *blank*

I ~~hear~~ the ~~loud~~ screams
   feel
inside me.

My heart ~~races.~~ ∧
              pounds

Transfer Your Learning

Across the Strands

Media Literacy: Successful ads use precise words and effective synonyms to show, not tell. Why does this approach work so well?

Across the Curriculum

Science and Technology: Think about the word choices you make when you write a science report. How are these choices different from when you write a story?

Talk About It

When you hear the word *dragon*, do you think of a frightening or friendly creature?

A Dragon's Lament

Poem by Jack Prelutsky

Word Choice

Use precise words and choose the right synonym. Jack Prelutsky uses the word *ferocious* here. What other word could he use? Why is *ferocious* a good word choice?

Word Choice

Show, don't tell. What lines show you the dragon may have earned his reputation?

Word Choice

Cross out unnecessary words. In a poem, every word has to pull its weight. Which words or lines in this poem work particularly well?

I'm tired of being a dragon,
Ferocious and brimming with flame,
The cause of unspeakable terror
When anyone mentions my name.

I'm bored with my bad reputation
For being a miserable brute,
And being routinely expected
To brazenly pillage and loot.

I wish that I weren't repulsive,
Despicable, ruthless, and fierce,
With talons designed to dismember
And fangs finely fashioned to pierce.

I've lost my desire for doing
The deeds any dragon should do,
But since I can't alter my nature,
I guess I'll just terrify you.

Reflecting

Reading Like a Writer: Choose one adjective from the poem that you thought was really effective. How did that adjective help you picture the dragon?

Metacognition: How does thinking about the poet's word choice affect your response to the poem?

Critical Literacy: What does the poet hope to achieve with this poem? Is it effective? Why or why not?

Talk About It
What makes a movie really scary?

The Usher

Poem by Mel Glenn

Did you see that movie where
The monster ate the alien
Who chopped up the zombie
Who decapitated the creature
Who strangled the werewolf
Who tore apart the giant spider?
I saw it.
Forty-seven times.
And I'm gonna see it forty-seven more times.
It's our biggest hit of the year.
I can hardly wait for the sequel.
If my own life is boring,
A safe, slow boat ride down
A well-marked channel,
Let my movies bring me to the places
Where the wild waves crash against the rocks.
Time for the next show?
Let it roll.
If I can't live it,
At least I'll see it.

"It could be the most terrifying motion picture
I have ever made!"— *Alfred Hitchcock*

"...and
remember,
the next
scream
you hear
may be
your own!"

**ALFRED
HITCHCOCK'S
"The Birds"**
TECHNICOLOR®

POSTERWIRE.COM

STARRING
**ROD TAYLOR · JESSICA TANDY
SUZANNE PLESHETTE** *and Introducing* **'TIPPI' HEDREN**
Based on Daphne Du Maurier's Classic Suspense Story!
Screenplay by EVAN HUNTER · Directed by ALFRED HITCHCOCK

A Fascinating
New Personality

Reflecting

Reading Like a Writer: Think about the effect the poet was hoping to achieve with the line "A safe, slow boat ride down/A well-marked channel...." How else could the poet have described everyday life?

Critical Literacy: Identify the spot in the poem where the title makes sense to you. Is "The Usher" the best title for this poem?

Connecting to Other Media: Think about different movie posters. What elements do designers include when they create a movie poster? Why?

Talk About It

Overcoming a fear of the unknown can lead to amazing adventures.

Scaredy Squirrel

Picture Book by Mélanie Watt

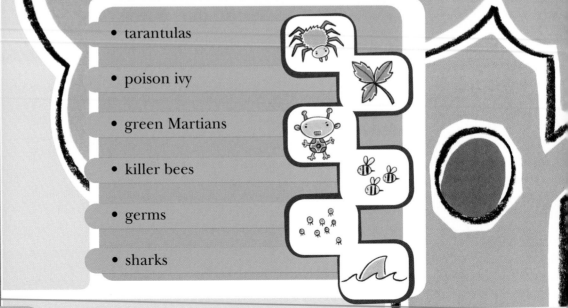

Scaredy Squirrel never leaves his nut tree. He'd rather stay in his safe and familiar tree than risk venturing out into the unknown. The unknown can be a scary place for a squirrel.

A few things Scaredy Squirrel is afraid of:

- tarantulas

- poison ivy

- green Martians

- killer bees

- germs

- sharks

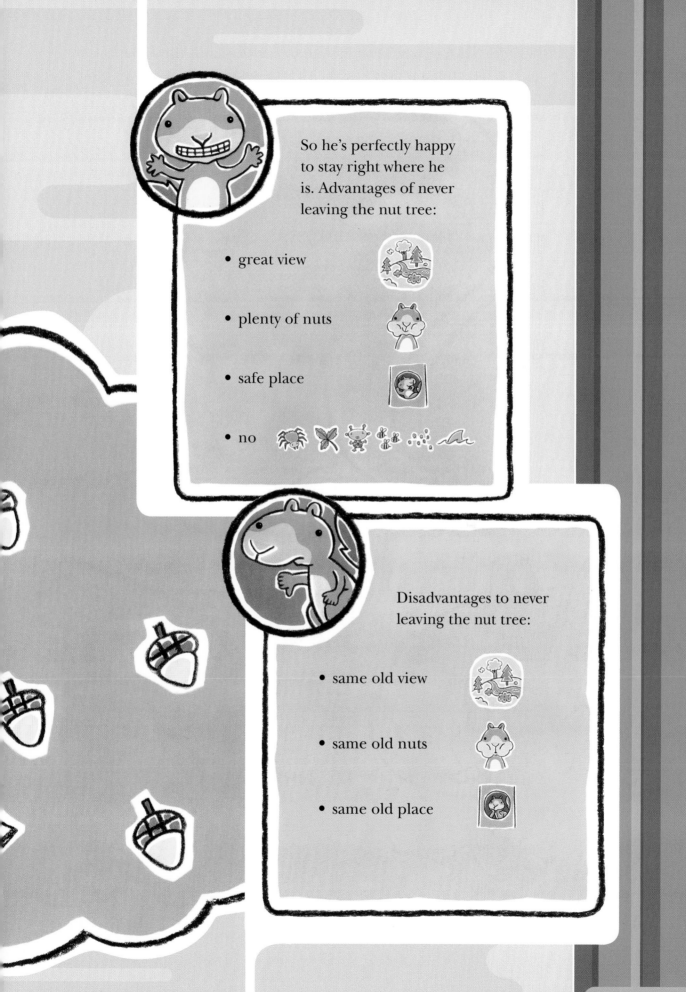

So he's perfectly happy to stay right where he is. Advantages of never leaving the nut tree:

- great view

- plenty of nuts

- safe place

- no

Disadvantages to never leaving the nut tree:

- same old view

- same old nuts

- same old place

In Scaredy Squirrel's nut tree, every day is the same. Everything is predictable. All is under control.

Scaredy Squirrel's daily routine:

6:45 a.m.	wake up
7:00 a.m.	eat a nut
7:15 a.m.	look at view
12:00 noon	eat a nut
12:30 p.m.	look at view
5:00 p.m.	eat a nut
5:31 p.m.	look at view
8:00 p.m.	go to sleep

BUT let's say, just for example, that something unexpected DID happen…. You can rest assured that this squirrel is prepared. A few items in Scaredy Squirrel's emergency kit:

- parachute
- bug spray
- mask and rubber gloves
- hard hat
- antibacterial soap
- calamine lotion
- net
- Band-Aid
- sardines

What to do in case of an emergency
according to Scaredy Squirrel:

Step 1: Panic

Step 2: Run

Step 3: Get kit

Step 4: Put on kit

Step 5: Consult Exit Plan

Step 6: Exit tree (if there is absolutely,
definitely, truly no other option)

EXIT PLAN – TOP SECRET

Exit 1: Note to self: Watch out for green Martians and
killer bees in the sky.

Exit 2: Note to self: Do not land in river. If unavoidable,
use sardines to distract sharks.

Exit 3: Note to self: Look out for poison ivy and for
tarantulas roaming the ground.

Exit 4: Note to self: Keep in mind that germs are
everywhere.

REMEMBER, IF ALL ELSE FAILS, PLAYING DEAD
IS ALWAYS A GOOD OPTION!

With his emergency kit in hand, Scaredy Squirrel
watches. Day after day he watches, until one day....

Thursday, 9:37 a.m. A killer bee appears! Scaredy
Squirrel jumps in panic, knocking his emergency kit
out of the tree. This was NOT part of the Plan. Scaredy
Squirrel jumps to catch his kit. He quickly regrets this
idea. The parachute is in the kit.

But something incredible happens....

He starts to glide. Scaredy Squirrel is no ordinary squirrel. He's a FLYING squirrel! He feels overjoyed! Adventurous! Scaredy Squirrel forgets all about the killer bee, not to mention the tarantulas, poison ivy, green Martians, germs, and sharks. Carefree! Alive! Until he lands in a bush ...

And plays DEAD.

30 minutes later....

1 hour later....

2 hours later....

Finally Scaredy Squirrel realizes that nothing horrible is happening in the unknown today. So he returns to his nut tree.

All this excitement has inspired Scaredy Squirrel to make drastic changes to his life.

Scaredy Squirrel's new-and-improved daily routine:

6:45 a.m.	wake up
7:00 a.m.	eat a nut
7:15 a.m.	look at view
9:37 a.m.	jump into the unknown
9:45 a.m.	play dead
11:45 a.m.	return home
12:00 noon	eat a nut
12:30 p.m.	look at view
5:00 p.m.	eat a nut
5:31 p.m.	look at view
8:00 p.m.	go to sleep

poison ivy

P.S. As for the emergency kit, Scaredy Squirrel is in no hurry to pick it up just yet.

Reflecting

Reading Like a Writer: Think about the different words for *fear* or *afraid* the writer uses. What other words could she have used?

Metacognition: How effective do you think you are at choosing the best word when you write? What can you do to improve your word choice?

Critical Thinking: This picture book is intended for young children but many older people like it as well. What aspects or features of the text do you find appealing?

How to **Summarize While Listening**

When you're listening to a speech, a news report, or dialogue in a movie, you may not want to take notes. So it's important to pay attention and figure out the speaker's main idea to help you summarize the key points.

Ask yourself:

- What is the speaker's topic? For example, it could be fear of public speaking.

- What is the speaker trying to tell you about that topic? That is, what is the message or main idea of the whole text? Sometimes, a speaker states the main idea in the first couple of sentences. Sometimes the main idea is not stated explicitly, and you have to infer the main idea by listening to everything the speaker says.

- What details support the main idea? It's not important to remember all the details, but you should try to remember a couple.

- What details are not important to the main idea? Some details may be included just to entertain the listener.

- What is the speaker's point of view or tone? How does it affect your understanding of the text/topic? For example, if a speaker lists the top ten things he likes to do, but his tone is sarcastic, then you know it's really a top-ten list of things he hates to do.

FEAR!

Speech by Martine

Imagine you're about to speak to a room full of people. Do you freeze with fear? That's sort of my problem. I freeze if I have to speak English to people I don't know. I grew up in Québec, speaking French all the time. It's only the last two years I started to learn English. You can hear I have an accent. Sometimes I make mistakes with words. So when I have to ask a stranger a question, I sometimes feel so afraid I can't speak. Luckily, I have lots of friends and family I can speak English to. And I have a lot to say! So, slowly, the fear of speaking is leaving me.

Transfer Your Learning

Across the Strands

Reading: How is summarizing as you listen similar to summarizing as you read? How is it different?

Across the Curriculum

History: Why would summarizing be an effective listening strategy in your history class?

Talk About It

Some people love rides. Some people just have to ride their fear to prove they're not afraid.

RIDE THE FEAR

Monologues by Deborah Karczewski

Summarizing →

Identify the speaker's topic. From the title "Ride the Fear" and the subtitle "Ferris Wheel," what do you think is the topic for the first monologue?

Summarizing →

Identify the speaker's main idea. What is this speaker's main idea?

Summarizing →

Identify the details that support the speaker's main idea and the details that are not important. What details in this paragraph are important? What details can you ignore?

Ferris Wheel – Monologue Number One

It's bad enough that those friends of mine dared me to go on this Monster Ferris Wheel when they know how much I hate heights … but to top it off, the ticket guy cut the ride line right behind me! That means *I'm* up here … and those sorry excuses for friends are way … way … way … down there! Aaaahhh!

I'm not happy! This car I'm riding in goes up and up and up and up … and just when I feel comfortable … I fall down and down and down! It's never-ending! I really regret having a funnel cake appetizer, cotton candy dinner, and snow cone dessert! *Yow!* Every time the Ferris wheel goes down, my stomach stays up!

It serves me right! If I hadn't screamed so much on the Tilt o'Whirl, they'd never have gotten the idea to dare me to go on this *rusty* machine of doom! Me and my big mouth! I didn't want to look like a *total* baby, y'know. I had already said "No way" to the roller coaster and "You're outta your mind" to the Loop the Loop! It was between the Monster Wheel and the Tower of Terror. They dared me to pick one or be named the group scaredy cat. I had no choice!

What's wrong with going to a carnival and playing safe little games like Ring Toss or Duck Pond? Who says real men ride death machines? I admit it! I'm a coward! Sue me!

Ooooohhh boy! Here we go again! Up and up and up! Moment at the top to breathe. And then … Aaaahhhhh!

Speed Demon — Monologue Number Two

Summarizing

Look for clues that reveal the speaker's tone and point of view. How does understanding this speaker's tone help you understand her main idea? Note that this is a different speaker with a different point of view.

I'm going to be a race-car driver … or maybe a motorcycle driver … or race a speed boat! Whatever, I can guarantee it's going to be *fast!* I feel alive when I'm *speeding*. Take roller coasters, my friends are scared to *death* on the steep downhill drops and I've got my arms in the air, cheering my head off! Feeling the wind whipping past me … it's like … *freedom!*

What about sledding? *Swooping* past the trees! Everything looks like stripes of colour *zipping* by. Little bits of ice sting my face, but it doesn't really hurt. It's so … *wild!*

I want to try bungee jumping! *Yeah!* Or — or whitewater rafting! Cool! Or — skydiving!

The *closest* I get to that feeling of speed these days is riding my bike, but it just doesn't make my heart pound. If I ride without touching the handlebars or I pop a wheelie, my mom says I'm tempting fate. She says that in order to enjoy life to the fullest, I have to *slow* down …. *Parents!*

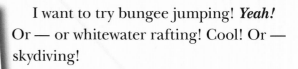

Reflecting

Summarizing: In four sentences, summarize either "Ferris Wheel" or "Speed Demon."

Metacognition: For the monologue you chose to summarize, what clues helped you identify the main idea? As a speaker, what do you do to help your listeners identify the main idea?

Critical Literacy: Both monologues reflect different points of view about rides. Which speaker do you find it easier to connect with? Why?

Talk About It
How often do you worry about things you don't need to worry about?

I Know I Flunked the History Test

Script by Peg Kehret

CAST: KAREN and HEIDI.
SETTING: Hallway of school.
KAREN and HEIDI enter. Each carries a file folder.

KAREN: I can't look. It's too painful.

HEIDI: Well, I'm looking. (*She opens her folder and lets out a whoop of delight.*) I got an A! That means I'll get an A in history.

KAREN: (*Glumly*) Congratulations.

HEIDI: I really studied for this one.

KAREN: I'll probably be grounded for the rest of the month.

HEIDI: Why? How did you do?

KAREN: I failed!

HEIDI: How do you know? You haven't looked yet.

KAREN: There's an F inside this folder. A big, red F.

HEIDI: But you studied, didn't you?

KAREN: What good would it do? I never get good grades in history. There's something wrong with my memory.

HEIDI: Even if you didn't study for the test, I doubt if you failed it. You came to class every day. You must remember something.

KAREN: I think my memory problem comes from eating too much turkey. There's some kind of enzyme in turkey that makes you stupid.

HEIDI: Where in the world did you hear that?

KAREN: Did you ever hear of a smart turkey? They're the most stupid creatures you can imagine.

HEIDI: Forget about the turkey and look at your grade.

KAREN: I never took such a hard test. All those questions about the War of 1812. Who cares where battles were fought so long ago? When my folks find out I flunked the history test, I'll be lucky if I only get grounded. They'll probably disown me.

HEIDI: Your parents are not likely to disown their only daughter. And you're not likely to get an F on the test. You've never had an F on any other test, have you?

KAREN: There's a first time for everything. Besides, Mr. Williams hates me.

HEIDI: Why do you think that?

KAREN: He just does. I can tell by the way he squints at me.

HEIDI: Mr. Williams squints at everyone. I think he needs glasses.

KAREN: It's different when he squints at me. At you, he squints benevolently. At me, he squints maliciously.

HEIDI: You are imagining things. Mr. Williams has no reason to hate you.

KAREN: Yes, he does. He hates me because I flunked the test.

HEIDI: Let's look at your test. Then you can worry about whether Mr. Williams hates you. *(She reaches for KAREN'S folder. KAREN jerks it away.)* If there was an award for negative attitude, you would win it.

KAREN: There! You see? Even my best friend agrees that I'm a loser.

HEIDI: Would you please open your folder and find out what your grade is? *(KAREN clutches folder to her chest and shakes her head.)* Do you want me to look for you?

KAREN: I don't need to look. I already know what my grade is.

HEIDI: How could you? Mr. Williams just handed these to us three minutes ago.

KAREN: I know what my grade is.

HEIDI: Really? *(KAREN nods yes.)* Are you telling me that you really did get an F? You aren't just worrying?

KAREN: You know the old saying that history repeats itself? Well, in my case, I'll be repeating history.

HEIDI: Oh. I'm sorry. Did Mr. Williams call your parents?

KAREN: No.

HEIDI: Then how did you find out?

KAREN: He didn't need to call. I knew the minute I got to the questions about the war that I was doomed.

HEIDI: *(Losing patience)* Have you seen your grade or haven't you?

KAREN: I don't need to see it. I told you, I already—*(HEIDI suddenly grabs KAREN'S test out of her hands.)* Hey! Give me that. *(HEIDI quickly opens folder and looks inside.)*

HEIDI: You got a C-plus.

KAREN: What? No way.

HEIDI: See for yourself. *(She holds the open folder under KAREN'S nose.)* A big, red C and a big, red plus.

KAREN: Mr. Williams must have made a mistake. I think he needs glasses.

HEIDI: There's a note, too. It says, "If you would study for these tests, you could probably get an A."

KAREN: I knew it. He got my folder mixed up with someone else's.

HEIDI: All that worrying for nothing. Come on. We don't want to be late for math.

KAREN: It doesn't matter if I'm late or not. I'm flunking math anyway. *(HEIDI rolls eyes in disgust. They exit.)*

Reflecting

Summarizing: If you were listening to this dialogue as you watched the play, how would you summarize it?

Metacognition: How does listening to a text rather than reading it affect your ability to summarize?

Critical Literacy: How are students depicted or represented in this dialogue? How are teachers depicted? Are those depictions accurate?

How to ▶ Identify Point of View

Most media texts are not neutral. They have a purpose. Two common purposes are to sell a product or to send a message.

Selling a Product

One common example of media texts that try to sell you something are ads. Whether it is a TV commercial for an iPod or a trailer at the local theatre, the ad is trying to sell something. Media texts that try to sell something may be created from the point of view of the advertiser or from the point of view of the consumer for that product. Such media texts usually present the positive side of a product.

> **point of view:** the position or attitude of one person, group, or agency toward a specific topic; for example, people who are afraid of snakes have a different point of view about a local zoo's snake exhibit than the person in charge of feeding the snakes.

NEGATIVE IONS = POSITIVE VIBES

FASHION®
NEGATIVE ION INFUSED
BRACELETS

BELIEVE IT OR NOT...

Negative ions are invisible, odourless molecules that are believed to increase energy, relieve stress, and enhance your mood. These bracelets are certified to contain negative ions, but most importantly, are certifiably fashionable!

FASHIONANGELS
ENTERPRISES

CALL 1.800.49.BEADS
FOR A STORE NEAR YOU.

Sending a Message

Some media texts are not created to sell a product but to send a message or to "sell" an idea. Anti-smoking ads or pro-peace stickers are good examples. If a song is about saving the whales and planting trees, that song is not neutral. Its purpose is to convince the listener that saving the environment is a good idea. The point of view of the songwriter is that saving the environment is a positive thing.

Media texts that try to send a message usually reflect the point of view of the person who created that text. These media texts may present only one point of view or several.

When you view or listen to a media text, ask:

- What is the purpose of this media text?

- What is the message of this media text?

- Do I agree with that message? What is my own opinion?

- Whose point of view is reflected here?

- Whose point of view is not reflected or missing?

Transfer Your Learning

Across the Strands

Writing: In writing, the trait of voice is closely connected to the concept of "point of view." How might the voice of an author writing from the point of view of a teenager be different from the voice of an author writing from the point of view of a grandparent?

Across the Curriculum

History: Why is it important to identify point of view when you examine photos or illustrations in history class?

Talk About It
What does this title mean to you?

Feel the Fear

Spoken Word by Michelle Muir

Identifying Point of View →

Identify the purpose of the media text. Some media texts sell an idea, some sell a product. Read the title and byline and think about why someone creates a spoken word piece.

Identifying Point of View →

Identify the message in the media text. At this point, what message is this text sending? Do you agree or disagree with it?

I read once that
Courage is not the absence of fear
But rather the understanding
That there is something more important than fear.
Now, the sometimes me wants to run and hide from everything
But the me I want the world to see
The me I wish to be … you know … the brown sugar
   wonder woman with the courage cape?
Yeah, well that she
Tells me
To remember who I be.
She tells me to remember all the things more important
   than my fear
She tells me to remember all the things I hold near and dear.

and Do It Anyway

My family
My friends
My past, present and future successes
Really good books
Warm weather recesses
Every class I ever taught
Every CD I ever bought
My poetry
My poetry
My poetry
So I take a deep breath,
Tie my courage cape on a little tighter
And go do the thing.

Identifying Point of View

Identify the point of view in the media text. Whose point of view is reflected in this text? Do you share the same point of view?

Identifying Point of View

Think about any points of view not reflected in the media text. Is there more than one point of view reflected? Is it necessary for this type of text to reflect a point of view other than the author's? Why or why not?

Reflecting

Point of View: Now that you have read the whole text, what message do you think it sends? How do you feel about this message?

Critical Literacy: How do you think others would feel about this message? Who would disagree with this author's message?

Metacognition: How does thinking about the author's message help you understand the point of view in this media text?

Talk About It
If you're afraid, can you still behave bravely?

Mona Parsons

A Courageous Canadian
Transcript from Histor!ca Minutes

CANADIANS LIBERATE HOLLAND 1945

Opening scene: Pan across war-torn area, with Canadian soldiers, tanks, and jeeps

On screen: **Canadians liberate Holland, 1945**

Camera focuses in on Sergeant directing a bedraggled woman towards the camera.

MONA: No, no, no! I tell you, I was in a German prison camp for four years.

SOLDIER 1: What's going on here, Sergeant?

SOLDIER 2: Claims she's a Canadian, sir, but … *(leans in and whispers)* she could be a German spy.

THE GESTAPO GOT ME.

SOLDIER 1 *(as other officer approaches)*: What's your name, lady?

MONA: Mona Parsons.

HARRY: Mona Parsons? From Wolfville—it's me, Harry Foster.

MONA: *(gasps)* Harry Foster!

HARRY: What happened to you?

MONA *(as they begin to walk together)*: I was in the resistance. The Gestapo got me...

Flashback: Mona standing in front of a German officer sitting at a desk.

Officer speaking in German, the following text appears as subtitles:
The penalty is death by firing squad.

Mona, standing proudly before court, speaking in German, the following text appears as subtitles:
Gentlemen. Good morning.

Cut to: Mona being escorted away by a German soldier. They are intercepted by the officer who declared her sentence.

OFFICER *(in English now)*: Dear lady, you have great courage. I recommend you appeal the sentence. *(he clicks his heels and bows his head to her)*

NARRATOR: Living in Holland during the war, Mona Parsons had helped downed allied airmen get back to Britain.

On screen: **A part of our heritage**

MONA: I will escape.

NARRATOR: And she did escape, and back in Nova Scotia after the war, she married General Harry Foster.

I WILL ESCAPE.

Reflecting

Identifying Point of View: Whose point of view is this selection told from? What message does this selection send?

Metacognition: Do you have enough background knowledge about World War II to understand this selection? What questions do you ask yourself as you read this text?

Critical Literacy: Histor!ca Minutes are short films (a minute long) that capture a moment in Canadian history. Their purpose is to celebrate Canadian history, to inform us, and to get us interested in it. Why is it important to keep that in mind as you read or view a Histor!ca Minute?

Nonfiction Recount

A nonfiction recount describes one event or a series of events. Nonfiction recounts usually

- begin with background information (so that the reader knows who was involved, and when and where the events took place)
- retell events in the order in which they happened
- use the past tense
- include the author's or character's thoughts or feelings
- give precise details so the reader can visualize the situation
- use transition words such as *after, before, during, finally, next,* and *then*

Recount text pattern may be used for true stories, news articles, or autobiographies. Recounts may be told using first person or third person. As you read recount text pattern, ask yourself: What events are being described? How is the pattern revealed?

Organizer

event ❯ event ❯ event

Transfer Your Learning

Across the Strands

Oral Communication: What have you learned about recount that can help you tell a story about something that happened to you?

Across the Curriculum

Health: What characteristics of recount make it an appropriate choice for an article about one person's efforts to stop smoking? Would another text pattern be more appropriate?

UNDERSTANDING

TEXT

PATTERNS

▶ Nonfiction Recount

Nonfiction Recount
Text Pattern
→

A nonfiction recount describes an event or a series of events. From the title, what events do you think will be described?

Nonfiction Recount
Text Pattern
→

Recounts usually begin with background information. What do you learn in this section that answers the questions who, where, and when?

Talk About It
What does it take to survive alone in the Arctic?

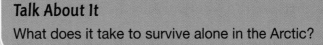

FIRE AND DEATH

**True Story by
Yvonne Galitis**

Lydia Mari Barragan discovered terror in the Arctic one horrible July night in 1987. Lydia and her fiancé, Jean-Jacques LeFrancq, were camping on an island in the Northwest Territories. The camp was located on the north shore of a large island on an isolated lake. There was no one else close to their location. Lydia and Jean-Jacques had no way of contacting anyone. They didn't expect to see another person until their pilot came back to pick them up.

They were enjoying their time together as they studied migrating caribou. Everything was going well, until one night a storm suddenly filled the sky with lightning.

The sun hovered just above the horizon, casting a subdued light. Lightning illuminated the sky even more. Smoke was blowing across the sky. The acrid odour of burning evergreen needles filled the air. Lydia and Jean-Jacques knew there was a fire, but they didn't know how much of the island was burning. Was it just one small area? A few isolated trees?

Lydia and Jean-Jacques took their canoe out on the lake to investigate. The entire island was on fire! They were in a tight spot, but not yet a desperate situation; they had time to get their gear and paddle over to the mainland. They would need to make two trips to get all their supplies across. If they didn't panic, they would be OK.

On their first trip, they took the tent and clothing. When they returned to their camp, the fire seemed to have slowed. A river that crossed the island contained the fire just short of their camp. Still, the smoke was horrible, and they could hear the snap of the flames. They reloaded their canoe with the rest of their supplies.

As they worked, the fire flared up. It leapt across the river and blazed toward their camp. Lydia and Jean-Jacques quickly finished loading the canoe and pushed back into the lake. They were spurred on by the roar of the fire and the sound of trees exploding with the intensity of the heat.

The heat of the fire caused a strong wind to blow toward the lake. Suddenly, Lydia and Jean-Jacques had more to fear from rising waves than from fire. Minutes after pushing off, their canoe was swamped and overturned. Despite being tossed into the freezing water, Lydia and Jean-Jacques were able to reach the canoe and cling to it as it pitched about in the rough water. But they couldn't turn the canoe over. Lydia and Jean-Jacques knew they couldn't waste any time on the canoe. They had to swim for shore.

→

Nonfiction Recount Text Pattern

Recounts usually retell events in order, using the past tense. What event is being described here? As you read, think about what is happening to Lydia. Visualize what happens as a flow chart of events.

At first, Lydia could hear Jean-Jacques encouraging her. Then she heard him choking and thrashing behind her. She tried desperately to reach him, but he kept slipping away. He was gone and she couldn't find him.

Shocked and filled with despair, Lydia tried not to panic. She feebly moved her arms and legs, trying to remain above the water. Worry, heartache, cold, and panic sapped her energy. Time passed in a dark haze of terror, misery, and grief, but still she felt the need to survive.

Unaware of time, Lydia soon stumbled on the stones of an unknown shore, unsure how she had made it there. She was in a life-threatening state of shock. Lydia allowed herself to think about losing Jean-Jacques. In horrified response to her loss, she cried out "Jean-Jacques! No-no-no-no!" Now she had no one…. She moved to a state beyond terror, beyond hunger, cold, exhaustion, and grief. She put those feelings away, knowing that if she did not, she would not survive. She was still determined to survive.

To survive, Lydia knew she had to walk over 110 km south across the tundra to a small outpost. The land would be covered in bug-filled swamps and thick forest. She might encounter wolves or polar bears. She would have only the food she could forage—roots and berries—and a bit of rice. Luckily, Lydia had found the first load of supplies they had brought over. Besides the rice, she also had warm clothes, insect repellent, boots, a compass, a lighter, and a map.

← **Nonfiction Recount Text Pattern**

Recounts often include the author's or character's thoughts or feelings. How well does the author describe Lydia's feelings?

← **Nonfiction Recount Text Pattern**

Recounts often give precise details so the reader can visualize the situation. What details in this section increase your understanding of the story?

Lydia's journey across the tundra was difficult. Despite the insect repellent, the bugs would not leave her alone. Her compass, because she was so close to the North Pole, didn't work properly. By chance, Lydia found an old trail to follow. She learned that no matter what obstacle covered that trail—stream, pond, or frigid mud—she had to follow the trail or risk getting lost. She waded across freezing streams and struggled through mud, keeping her eyes on the trail and her ears open for animals.

Unfortunately, the trail ended before she reached civilization. As Lydia tried to work out what to do, she caught sight of a bear a few metres away in the trees. She froze, telling herself not to move, not to panic. The bear sniffed the air but didn't move. After several terrifying moments, it wandered away.

As the days passed, Lydia kept reminding herself to stay calm. She was exhausted. She was running out of rice. She had blisters and bug bites. She wasn't even sure she was heading in the right direction. She fought feelings of uncertainty and anxiety and kept on walking. She couldn't give up or give in to her fear.

Shortly after she ran out of rice, Lydia came across a log cabin. The door was unlocked and there was a small bit of food inside. Lydia decided to spend a few days in the cabin to allow her feet to heal. Staying, she could also avoid the wolf that had suddenly appeared outside the cabin.

Five days later, as Lydia was writing a note for the cabin's owners, she heard a boat! Her horrifying ordeal was over with the arrival of Gene-Marie Oudzi. Gene-Marie was surprised to see Lydia. No one had ever arrived at the cabin by foot before. Lydia had crossed more than 100 km of tundra.

Lydia's Arctic nightmare taught her she had the courage to survive. It taught her the importance of staying calm when all you want to do is panic.

Nonfiction Recount Text Pattern

→

Recounts often use transition words that show the order of events. What word in this paragraph clearly shows the order of events?

Reflecting

Analyzing Text Patterns: What events are described in this recount? Does the author give you enough information about events for you to understand what happened to Lydia? What else would you want to know about what happened to her?

Metacognition: How does understanding the characteristics of nonfiction recount help you better understand this selection?

Critical Literacy: How would this true story be different if it were told in the first person by Lydia?

Talk About It

In this true story, the author and her husband barely survive a bear attack. What other survival stories do you know?

YOU ARE IN BEAR COUNTRY

True Story by Patricia Van Tighem from *The Bear's Embrace*

The narrow valley stretches dark green and white ahead, with soft grey cloud close above. What a contrast to yesterday's early brightness. Trevor's blue anorak and orange backpack move brightly ahead of me. He waits at the steepest parts of the trail to give me a hand.

It doesn't take long to cover this part of the trail. The sound of Trevor's singing up ahead makes me glad. "Blue skies smiling at me, nothing but blue skies do I see…."

He's gone around a bend now and is obscured from sight by trees. I quicken my step to rejoin him. The trail has widened, and we could walk beside each other, hold hands, and talk.

A bear.

And Trevor.

Two more steps forward. I stop. A bear? From the side. Light brown. A hump. A dish-shaped face.

A grizzly. Charging. And Trevor. Fast. He half turns away. The bear's on him, its jaws closing around his thigh, bringing him down.

Seconds pass. Time holds still.

A grizzly?

I take two steps back. Where am I going? What should I do? My heart beats loud in the silent, snowy woods. I can't outrun a bear. It knows I'm here. I can't leave Trevor. Panic rising. How will I get past the bear? Trevor? My mind racing. Legs like jelly. Shaky, weak. Think.

The bear has Trevor. I can't see anything because of the bushes. I can't hear anything.

Not a bear!

I can't run. Take off my pack. It might divert the bear. After summers of handing out "You Are in Bear Country" pamphlets at the Banff Park gates, instructions for a bear encounter flash through my brain. I throw my pack down. So fast. My mind whirling.

Climb a tree.

Grizzlies can't climb trees. Nor can I! I have to. A tree with small, dry branches all the way up; right beside me. Get up! Steady and slow, shaking. Don't fall. Don't break the branches. They get smaller the higher I go. I have to stop. I feel very high. The branches are thin. Can't go higher. Stop climbing. Look down.

Trevor?

Scared. Snow falling. Soft. Absolute quiet.

I freeze. Terror fills me. It's right there. Eye contact. Small bear eyes in large brown furry head, mouth open. It's charging the tree. A scream, loud. It's moving so incredibly fast. It can't. Grizzlies can't climb trees! Everything so fast. It launches itself at the tree. Three huge lunges, branches flying and cracking. Twenty feet up. I'm frozen. Up. Brown ball of muscle and fury. So fast. Another scream. Cut off. Knocks the branch out from beneath my feet. Swats at my leg. My mind folds in.

On the ground. What's happening? Protect my head. Which way is up? Roll on my front. Play dead, and it will go away. It will go away. Trevor and I are not supposed to die yet. Don't fight, make it worse. Be passive. Hold still. Tuck my chin in. I won't die. It will leave.

A grizzly is chewing on my head.

Crunch of my bones. Slurps. Heavy animal breathing. Thick animal smell. No pain. So fast. Jaws around my head. Not aggressive. Just chewing, like a dog with a bone. Go away! I'm holding still. Horror. I can't believe this. Scrape of teeth on skull. Which way is down, so I can put my face there? Slurping and crunching. Lolling my head in its jaws. Playing with my head.

I'm angry.

I don't want to die. Get lost, you stupid bear! My mother will be so sad. I don't want to be a tragic death. Everyone will cry. Thoughts flit through my head. Incredulous. Angry. Terrified. Helpless. The bear is doing so much damage. Crunch and scrape. Anger wants to explode from my head. I don't want to die.

One hand pinned under my head. Work fingers free. There's a huge, distorted black nose right there in front of me. My fingers reach to tweak it. Gently. A diversion. Don't want to make the bear more angry. Big and black and sensitive, like a dog's nose. Divert it from chewing on me. A light twist. Blurred view. Don't look now. A woof! It's backed off. Am I dead?

Open an eye. Peek. It's still there, pacing in front of me. Walks ten feet, turns. Swinging its head back and forth. Ten feet and turns. Looking at me. Low woofs. Little eyes, looking right at me. Quick, close my eye. Perfectly still.

Please make it go away.

Please make it go away.

Please make it go away.

Over and over in my head. How long?

❋ ❋ ❋ ❋ ❋ ❋ ❋ ❋ ❋ ❋ ❋ ❋

The room is hot. The nurses have finished my evening suture care, placing antibiotic ointment along the length of every suture line: across my scalp, over and over; across my nose and forehead and cheek; under my chin. I hate it. They are gone now, and I am alone, swollen and hurting.

But there are hands on my head. I hit at the air. Go away! Leave me alone! But no one is there. My hands cut through the space above my head. I'm frightened.

"Hello?"

No answer. I'm sure I heard someone come in, but no one answers.

The hands are there again. I hit at them. Nothing but air. Panic.

"Who's there?"

No answer. I curl up, back to the side rail. Don't touch me! I pull the covers up to my chin. Everything's black. I want to tear my face off, find my old one beneath so that I can see again.

"Hello?" Tentatively this time. Still no answer. Am I going crazy? Those hands, picking at and rubbing my head. They aren't really there. Be calm, Patricia. It's just sensations. I cower in my bed.

Something is in my room, even if I can't see it. Somebody help me! It must be the middle of the night. Frantically, I fight with the bed covers to find my call bell. There are hands all over me.

Almost immediately, there's a voice. A kind, female voice. A nurse. Eagerly, I turn my head towards her.

Oh no!

It is black all around my pit. The kind voice is a giant bat, hairy, black and brown. It hovers above me, wings open wide. Huge, shiny, black eyes. I feel myself shrink down into the bed. Whimpering.

"What's the matter?" the voice wants to know. "Do you need something?"

I can't talk. I feel mouth-dry horror. It's coming down on me, coming down into my pit. It's the length of my bed. What can I do? Shrivel into a ball. Away from that thing.

The voice is gone. The bat, too. I hear voices outside my room, in the hallway, then footsteps. I'm scared to raise my head. But I do. Help me.

I want to scream. There are two bats now, one on each side of my room, in the hallway, then footsteps. I'm scared to raise my head. But I do. Help me.

I want to scream. There are two bats now, one on each side of my bed, hovering above me. Expressionless, huge, hairy faces. Teeth. Black. The voices are sympathetic, soft. A small, warm hand cradles mine.

"What's the matter? Can you tell me?"

I want to disappear into the security of that voice. I try to talk, but I'm crying. The bats hover above me, staring. Enormous, quivering bodies.

I'm burning up. There's sudden confusion. The room is full of voices, up and down. My brother Gordon. My mother. The resident. He's changing the analgesic order, he says.

The room is filled with wide wings and faces with pointy, sharp teeth. Mom is real, I know. The bats aren't. I hear Mom's voice. I like it. I know that voice so well. Her small hands hold mine. I feel her wedding ring. The bats are there, but they are less threatening now.

The nurse is back with a needle. I don't want it. I'm agitated. Fearful. Hot. Yes, I hurt. Okay, if it won't make me wacky. If you're sure. I want to relax, leave the world behind.

Mom is here. And a pill, too. What is it? Never mind. I'll take it. And a fan. That's nice. Blow the heat away. Hold on to me, Mom, I don't know where I'm going. It's only early evening. I wish it were morning. I wish it were next month. Or last month.

The drugs carry me away. The bats are gone. I am just me again in my bed. Just me, sore and swollen and unable to see. It's black around and inside me. Quiet night, calm, cooler. Sleep.

Reflecting

Analyzing Text Patterns: What characteristics of recount text pattern does the author use? What makes a recount text pattern suitable for this selection?

Metacognition: Do you find it easy or hard to identify the characteristics of a particular text pattern? What can you do to improve your ability to identify text patterns?

Critical Literacy: What do you think motivated this author to write about her experiences of surviving a bear attack?

The reading strategy of summarizing can help you to better understand texts in other subject areas. As you read this article, identify its main idea and supporting details.

Bullies and Bytes

Online Article by Sabrina Yoong
Sponsored by the Royal Canadian Mounted Police

The Internet is part of day-to-day life. Politicians have Facebook profiles, grandparents have e-mail addresses, and the verb *to google* is in many dictionaries. Socializing with friends often includes online MSN conversations and Facebook comments; in fact, these are often the preferred way to make plans. The distinction between the Internet and everyday life has blurred in many ways, and it's not always positive.

In February of 2007, eleven high school students north of Toronto were suspended after posting negative comments online about their principal. The school administration determined that it was a case of cyber bullying, and the students were suspended for three to eight days each. In the same year, five eighth-graders were forbidden to go on their year-end trip because of negative comments they had posted on Facebook about teachers. Their actions were considered cyber bullying. Five students were suspended from another school after posting comments online about their vice-principal.

What exactly is cyber bullying? *Cyber bullying* is when someone uses tools such as text messaging, e-mail, instant messaging, or chat rooms to harass, intimidate, or antagonize another individual. Cyber bullying also includes *flame wars* (online discussions on a bulletin board or social network site that sink to a series of personal attacks). Some forms of cyber bullying can result in charges of criminal harassment or *defamatory libel* (the illegal publication of untrue material that exposes anyone to hatred, contempt, or ridicule).

Cyber bullying differs from traditional schoolyard bullying in a number of ways. The traditional bully is usually bigger and stronger than his or her victims and must be physically close to them in order to intimidate or antagonize. The cyber bully just needs access to the Internet or a cellphone. Although cyber bullying lacks the threat of immediate physical harm, the victims of cyber bullying are absolutely powerless against their attackers. If victims can't identify their bullies, it's hard to defend themselves. As well, cyber bullying often falls beyond the legal jurisdiction of schools. If students aren't bullying other students at school, administrators are often unsure if they have authority to deal with the bullying.

The students mentioned often didn't fit the profile of a traditional bully. One was a member of the student council and another was a varsity sports team member. It seems strange that these students would be involved with bullying, but the anonymity of the Internet means that people feel freer to say things online that they would never say face to face. People are often more cruel online, and because they never see their victim's reaction, they are much less likely to realize the impact of their actions.

Victims often resist reporting cyber bullying to adults for fear of having Internet privileges or cellphones taken away. When the Internet and cellphones are such important tools for communicating with your friends, the prospect of losing them is devastating. But there is a lot you can do when you've been the victim of cyber bullying. Never respond to harassing messages online; instead, block the user. Most websites have tools that allow you to report users who are abusive or who violate the terms of use by harassing other users. Sometimes it's as easy as clicking a "report abuse" link. But if that's not the case, there are still things you can do. It can be hard, but it's important to tell an adult you trust about what is going on. Make sure to save screen captures of offensive sites, and save chat room or instant messenger conversations. Inform your Internet service provider or cellphone service provider. They usually have terms of service agreements that prohibit users from harassing others online—it's just a matter of reporting cyber bullying so that something can be done.

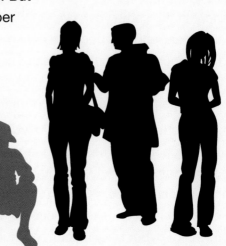
One in four kids is bullied

In order to prevent cyber bullying, be considerate when you're posting online. It sounds cheesy, but ask yourself, "Would I be okay with someone else saying this about me on the Internet for everyone to read?" Speak out when you see someone being mean to someone else on a bulletin board or in a chat room. Bullies respond better to criticism from someone they consider a peer than to disapproval from an adult. Cyber bullying can be scary, but remember that you have the right to feel safe and secure—both online and off.

Reflecting

Metacognition: How did summarizing this article help you understand it? What other strategies from the unit helped you understand this article?

Critical Literacy: From whose point of view is this article told? How effectively does the author capture that point of view? Is this article fair? Explain.

Selections Grouped by Theme and Form

Index

Credits

Charlie's Angels: Spelling-Goldberg/The Kobal Collection. 40 Cagney and Lacy: CBS-TV/The Kobal Collection. Stephanie Zimbalist: NBC-TV/The Kobal Collection Gillian Anderson: 20th Century Fox/The Kobal Collection/Morton, Merrick. S. Epatha Merkerson: Universal TV/Wolf Film/The Kobal Collection. 41 Marg Helgenberger: CBS-TV/The Kobal Collection. Klea Scott: Photographer: Michael Courtney. Glen Close: Fox-TV/The Kobal Collection. (fingerprint) Germán Ariel Berra/Shutterstock. 42–43 (Border) Shipov Oleg/Shutterstock. (Background) Connors Bros./Shutterstock 42–43 Kenneth Garrett/National Geographic Image Collection, all, except 42 (Cat scan of Tut's brain) University of Liverpool UK. 44 Laurence Gough/Shutterstock 45 (Background-sky) RobertWróblewski/Shutterstock. (Background-coast) Jaroslaw Grudzinski/Shutterstock. (map) © Worldspec/NASA/Alamy (sailboat) Daniel Gilbey/Shutterstock. 46 Philip Novess/Shutterstock. 46 Alan Smillie/Shutterstock. 47 (sea and sky composite) Peter Hendrie/Getty Images and Stephen Swinktek/Getty Images. 48–54 (Background-sea) ANP/Shutterstock. (Background journal) Kmitu/Shutterstock. 48 (maps) © Jack McMaster. (Sir John Franklin) © National Maritime Museum, London. 49 (John Rae and Inuit) Manitoba Archives for Hudson's Bay. 50 (Preparing Boats for Winter) © National Maritime Museum, London. 51 (Men Dragging Boats) © National Maritime Museum, London. (Tents in summer snowstorm) © Walt Kowal. 52 (Graves of three sailors) © Owen Beattie. 53 (Reconstructing graves) © Owen Beattie. 54 (British Explorers Dressed for Spring): Toronto Public Library, Toronto Reference Library (Baldwin Room). (Rusty can) © National Maritime Museum, London. 55 (Burial Service for one of Franklin's sailors) © Janet Wilson. 56 Vaide Seskauskiene/Shutterstock. 57 (periwinkles) Chelmodeev Alexander Vasilyevich/Shutterstock. (Crab) Nicholas James Homrich/Shutterstock. (aquarium) Teze/Shutterstock. 59 Stephen VanHorn/Shutterstock. 60 © Jupiter Images, 2007. 65-68 Trout 55/Shutterstock. 69 Associated Press. 72-81 (Background) Perov Stanislav/Shutterstock. 82 © iStockphoto.com/Yvonne Chamberlain. 83 (Background) SSilver/Shutterstcok. (Dragon) ussr/Shutterstock. 84-85 (Backgound) Gilmanshin/Shutterstock. 85 THE KOBAL COLLECTION. UNIVERSAL/THE KOBAL COLLECTION. 92 Charles Gupton/CORBIS. 93 Rebvt/Shutterstock. 94 (rollercoaster tracks) Xavier Pironet/Shutterstock. (people in rollercoaster) dwphotos/Shutterstock. 95—97 © Jupiter Images, 2007. 100-101 (Background) Jyothi Joshi/Shutterstock. (Background) Ali Mazraie Shadi/Shutterstock. 102-103 (Background) Shawn Talbot. (all) Courtesy—The Histor!ca Foundation of Canada.104 Galina Barskaya.105-108 Litwin Photography/Shutterstock. 114 © iStockphoto.com/Galima Barskaya.

Art

3–7 illustrated by Attila Adorjany. 16–21 illustrated by Harvey Chan. 23–25 illustrated by Chris Beatrice; tech art illustrated by Deborah Crowle. 28–29 Jake Bauming/Industrial Strength Graphics. 45–47 illustrated by Aleks Sennwald. 72–81 illustrated by Owen Sherwood, Ian Kim. 105–108 illustrated by Matthew Woodson. 109–113 illustrated by Jake Bauming/Industrial Strength Graphics.